Organic Beekeeping

Principles, Practices and Pitfalls

Grant F. C. Gillard

Organic Beekeeping:
Principles, Practices and Pitfalls

By Grant F.C. Gillard

Copyright 2015 Grant F.C. Gillard

For more information:

Grant F.C. Gillard
3721 North High Street
Jackson, MO 63755

gillard5@charter.net

Grant F.C. Gillard has been keeping bees since 1981. He speaks at bee conferences and conventions across the nation. To check his availability, contact him at gillard5@charter.net

You can find more information about the author at the conclusion of this book, or www.grantgillard.weebly.com

To order additional copies of this book:
https://www.createspace.com/5273543

For a full listing of Grant's manuscripts:
http://grantgillard.weebly.com/my-books.html

Dedication

In reality, we are the sum of all
those saints (and sinners) who have come before us
to show us the way, to ignite a passion for excellence
within our hearts, and to kindle in our deepest being
that a fire for learning.

I was blessed to have stumbled, perhaps
providentially, into a course on beekeeping called
"Entomology 222" in my sophomore year at Iowa
State University. I was merely looking for a
guaranteed, no-brainer course where I would get an
easy "A" as I sorely needed this kind of a course to
raise my grade point average after my freshman year.

My advisor, whose name I can't recall at this time,
ran through the course catalog and made several
suggestions. Nothing seemed to catch my interest
until he mentioned **Entomology 222: Beekeeping**,
which he quickly dismissed with a disparaging,

"But this class is for the granola crowd, you know,
the nuts and the flakes."

Little did he know that I was one of those "granola"-types. Little did I know my decision would set my life on a marvelous trajectory that would change my future and set in motion an unknown agenda that led me into an apicultural Promised Land.

The classroom instructor was Richard Trump, a retired, high school biology instructor and Presbyterian elder at the Collegiate Presbyterian Church where we both worshipped on Sunday mornings listening to the sermons of Rev. Harry Strong.

"Dr. Trump," as we called him, was a marvelous teacher. He only gave two grades for this course; an "A" or an "F." As we entered the University bee yard to inspect the hives, if we got stung, proving that we were working the hives, we received an "A." If we didn't get stung, we received an "F."

Needless to say, we all got "A's."

For his capable leadership and the incredible investment of time and energy he placed in us, this book is gratefully dedicated.

Mr. Trump passed away at the age of 98 on November 1, 2010.

Table of Contents

Foreword:

Organic is a labeling term that indicates that the food or other agricultural product has been produced through approved methods that integrate cultural, biological, and mechanical practices that foster cycling of resources, promote ecological balance, and conserve biodiversity. Synthetic fertilizers, sewage sludge, irradiation, and genetic engineering may not be used.

The labeling requirements of the NOP apply to raw, fresh products and processed products that contain organic agricultural ingredients. Agricultural products that are sold, labeled, or represented as organic must be produced and processed in accordance with the NOP standards.

Except for operations whose gross income from organic sales totals $5,000 or less, farm and processing operations that grow and process organic agricultural products must be certified by USDA-accredited certifying agents. However, even the operations exempt from certification must still adhere and comply with the regulations of the NOP.

The material drawn for this book is presumed to be accurate based on the current information available from the National Organic Program and the USDA at the time of its publication.

Its purpose is to guide the reader into considering the overwhelming obstacles that must be laid in place prior to using the word, "organic," to describe their apicultural operation. Without such compliance, producers and marketers are forbidden to use the word, "organic."

Chapter 1:

Introduction and Background

*"The irony of the organic movement
is that it attempts to reinvent
what we once had."*

A young lady approached my vendor booth at the Fall Conference of the Missouri State Beekeepers Association in October of 2014. As we conversed, she mentioned she was in her first year of beekeeping. I congratulated her and asked how many hives she started that spring. She replied, "Three, and we're trying to stay as natural as possible."

I think the key to her statement was the qualifier, *"as possible."* There is a growing segment in our beekeeping circles to move away from the traditional, chemical responses in favor of more natural options. Still, we wrestle with the nagging feeling that some treatments, of some kind, may be necessary to save our bees, and save them, namely, from the varroa mites.

But we're nervous about the possibilities of random, careless, and prophylactic chemical treatments allowing these pests to build a resistance to the treatments. Further, we don't like the idea of chemical residues taking up residence in our wax comb. And these problems are happening, right now.

In response to our nervous apprehension that beekeepers may be willing contributors to these problems, we began insisting on Integrated Pest Management, or IPM. The basic tenants of IPM require the beekeeper to monitor pest levels, determine an economic threshold, and treat when and if it's necessary.

But IPM takes work, time and energy. Larger beekeeping operations continue, out of necessity, to use the routine, prophylactic treatments as a proactive and preventative measure. But the collateral damage perpetuates an uneasy discontent, a longing for something better, something safer yet still effective. The pendulum began a graceful arc back to the side of more natural beekeeping management.

Almost across the board, the modern trend in beekeeping is shifting away from a dependency on chemicals, to a philosophy of, *"as natural as possible."* We still desire to keep our bees alive, perhaps conceding the necessity of minimal, occasional, as-needed chemical intervention. We seem to have compromised with the application of, "soft," chemicals or, "natural," treatments. But their efficacy remains in question, and they seem to involve more labor.

But such a shift has also generated several, creative, "kitchen sink," concoctions of ingredients like mentholyptus cough drops in the hive entrance and walnut shavings for our smokers.

Natural? Maybe. Safe and effective? Who the heck knows? Better than those horrible chemicals? Hmmmm.

When the topic of these off-beat, supposedly natural beekeeping remedies comes up in conversations at bee meetings, I'm reminded of a beekeeper who called me with an incredible discovery.

He told me he had six bee hives, situated in a right row, in his expansive back yard, at the rear of the property near the fence that backed up to a deep woods. One chilly fall day, he was exercising his dog in the back yard. The skies were overcast and the temperatures quite cool. The bees were not flying or taking cleansing flights, preferring to cluster inside the hive.

The dog excitedly ran around his master, sniffing the ground for scents left behind by the likes of rabbits and mice. The dog circled the row of hives, ceremoniously lifted his leg on the hive on the end, and proceeded to heedlessly empty his bladder on the side of the end hive.

The beekeeper thought nothing of it, until later that spring, as the first warm days began to stir the bees into activity. To his dismay, five of his six hives perished over the winter, the only surviving hive was the one which received the dog urine, "treatment."

He peppered me with ideas on why this hive survived, theories of salt content and urea levels in the urine, the fact that this dog was a neutered male. Did I think he had any marketable applications? Did I know any sources who would give him a financial grant to pursue his idea, maybe apply for a patent?

And he was serious. I tried not to laugh. Surely crazier notions have crossed the vacant minds of creative entrepreneurs and desperate beekeepers hoping to find a cure to the mysterious, disappearing bee disease, let alone making a buck or two. I suggested he continue his research and keep me posted.

I've not heard back from him. Perhaps the dog got stung when the weather moderated and learned to urinate in safer, bee-free areas of the yard. No doubt, many other worthy ideas have found their terminus when the research subjects refused to cooperate.

Without the yet undiscovered benefits of canine urine, our beekeeping industry moderates to more natural applications, even trying to rediscover the secret of the good old days prior to the arrival of the varroa mite when you could dump bees in a box, get out of their way, and effortlessly harvest monster crops of the best honey.

Taken to the extreme, some beekeepers eschew all treatments, of any kind, in what they call, "treatment-free," beekeeping. If the bee didn't bring it into the hive, then it does not belong there!

The more I talk to beekeepers, the more this trend of moving away from chemicals rings true. Many beekeepers would love to eliminate all treatments, natural or otherwise, and shift to this radical idea of being treatment-free. The ideal benefits are less labor, less expense, less intrusive inspections, less stress on the colony, but there will be hive mortality, more or less to various extents, and some of these losses could have been prevented with prudent usage of chemical treatments.

This is the trade-off, our modern conundrum, that without some kind of treatment, we can expect hive mortality that may have been preventable. But we're uncomfortable with the chemical treatments, residues and increasing resistance requiring stronger, more potent chemicals.

However, natural treatments and soft chemicals lack the efficacy we're looking for and take more labor...so there we are: stuck. We're like the baseball player wanting to steal second base but finds himself paralyzed with the fear of stepping off first base.

In my apiaries, I've always leaned on the more natural treatments, and I've been blessed with the information provided in Ross Conrad's book, *"Natural Beekeeping,"* (2nd Edition, 2013, Chelsea Green Publishing ISBN-13: 978-1603583626, ISBN-10: 1603583629, available on *www.amazon.com*).

I am, however, going to take exception to his subtitle, *"Organic Approaches to Modern Apiculture."* As we proceed through this manuscript, I'm going to insist we all get on the same page when it comes to the definition of this nebulous word, "organic." Just because it's, "natural," however you want to define THAT word, does not mean it's organic. Just because something is organic, does not mean it's safe or non-toxic.

As a beekeeper who has tried the treatment-free avenues of beekeeping, and in some years, suffered unconscionable losses, I confess I hate losing hives. "Hate," is a strong word, but it rings true with me. Especially in the spring, when I open a hive with ample stores and nothing but dead bees, I hate the idea I could have done something the previous fall. No, I hate the idea I SHOULD have done something the previous fall.

I hate losing production when I have to split a strong colony to replace a winter dead-out. I hate having to buy new packages or nucs the following spring to fill dead hives. I hate the inconvenience of searching, often in vain, for those elusive, early spring nucs, only to have the nuc producers chide me with the admonition, "Should have called me before Christmas. I'm all sold out."

I hate conceding the nuc producer's correct assessment, but, to my credit, I was planning on these hives surviving the winter, thank you.

I hate the lost production that a normally healthy, overwintered colony would have produced, had it survived, over and above what a replacement nuc or package is likely capable of producing. There is nothing with more potential than an overwintered colony.

Our present situations have us stuck between the proverbial rock and a hard place, trying to balance our desire for a simpler, perhaps, "more natural," resolution to our challenges, while acquiescing to the need to implement some chemical method of mite control that also comes with the attendant potential for collateral damage and potentially challenging side effects.

Back at the MSBA Fall Conference, I commended this young woman for selecting the natural option. I wished her well and hoped she enjoyed her bees as much as I do. I invited her to contact me if I could be of assistance, but I also said her first line of defense was finding a mentor in her local association.

She shrugged, and without much elaboration mentioned her local association seemed, "bent on promoting chemicals."

A Little Historical Background:

The past two decades in American beekeeping finds a growing divide between the stodgy, entrenched conventional beekeepers (traditionally advocating the responsible use of available pharmaceutical responses) against an idealistic, somewhat zealous uprising totally repulsed by the notion that these supposedly beneficial, potentially necessary treatments may be the very thing that are making our bees sick. Is the cure now worse than the disease?

We have research that strongly associates shocking side-effects with the legally-registered, approved, chemical treatments. We've discovered unintended, collateral consequences to queen fertility, semen quality in drones, worker bees and their susceptibility to viruses, and a growing suspicion that mites are becoming resistant to these same approved chemicals, basically rendering the treatments useless and expensive.

When one weapon in our thin, and thinning arsenal starts shooting blanks, we start looking for bigger artillery. But much of that bigger artillery has not yet made it to the front lines.

Since 2006, beekeepers have been reeling from a mysterious, multi-symptom syndrome devastating bee colonies we've coined as, "Colony Collapse Disorder," or CCD, for short. To this day, no one has found a single cause, the, "smoking gun," to which we can target our arsenal of chemical responses.

Some researchers are beginning to wonder if our routine, prophylactic administration of the approved chemicals may be a contributing factor to the advent of CCD. We're beginning to ponder if the chemicals to kill the mites may be decreasing the bee's immunity, making the colony susceptible to previously innocuous viruses.

Nevertheless, we've had no choice but to simply learn to deal with CCD and the increasing numbers of lost hives as we struggle through the repercussions, often trying in vain to keep our bees alive and our apicultural heads above water.

It's not just the survival of the honey bee that's at stake, but the potential livelihoods of commercial beekeepers and the consequential damage inflicted upon an agricultural production system which has grown dependent upon migratory pollination services. We're also beginning to question if the food system that depends upon our bees for its productivity might possibly be the same environment responsible for unheralded hive losses.

Not that we're going to change this production system overnight, but we're experiencing problems in the hive that ripple all through our food supply. Estimates credit the honey bee as responsible for one of every three bites of food on our plates, totaling $18 billion dollars worth of food every year. Newspaper headlines seasonally herald the problem of, "the bee shortage."

At this juncture, many people will pull out that quote from some guy named, "Einstein," who said, "If the bees disappear from the surface of the earth, humanity would have no more than four years to live. No more bees, no more pollination, no more people."

First, Albert Einstein is not the likely source of this quote, though it's always a good tactic to put fictitious words in the mouth of someone famous to elevate the status of the idea. Albert Einstein, the physicist, was not a beekeeper, nor an entomologist or a botanist, and the quote surfaced in 1994, long after his death in 1955, and searches of his writings reveal nothing close to this idea. We're pretty confident the quote did not originate with Albert Einstein, nor for that matter, anyone credible enough to lend credence to this idea.

Second, if all the bees died, we'd still have many wind-pollinated crops like corn, wheat, rice, potatoes...all those nice white, starchy, diabetes-accelerating foods. We would not starve, but we'd be missing a host of nutritious fruits and vegetables from our diet. Our livestock would still reproduce so we would not be forced into vegetarianism. Still, all things considered, we need to protect the honey bees for the sake of our food, our health and our future.

With the advent of CCD, and rounding up the usual, perceived suspects of GMO-grown crops and systemic pesticides, a new face of beekeeping arose. Hordes of young people, primarily, concerned about the news of the sudden decline of the bees hitting the front page of every form of media, stepped forward to take up the mantle of beekeeping, namely in an effort to, "save," the fragile honey bee. They thronged to local bee associations, clamoring for classes on how to begin keeping bees, claiming they, "had always wanted to keep bees."

A new segment in the apicultural industry, dubbed the, "backyard beekeeper," staked a unique prominence in conferences and publications. A perceptible disturbance in the force was felt.

With the perception that the fragile honey bee could not survive on her own, with the suspicion that normal applications of legally-registered pesticides were to chiefly to blame, a newfound aspect to keeping honey bees emerged on the front lines. "Natural," and, "organic," beekeeping became hot topics at bee meetings and conferences, drawing record attendance numbers.

Alternatives to the conventional, "Langstroth," hive, namely, "Warre hives," and, "top bar hives," even, "hex hives," caught manufacturer's attention. Unconventional managerial options of, "treatment-free beekeeping," and, "chemical-free beekeeping," challenged the traditional, prophylactic pharmaceutical protocols.

The face of beekeeping experienced a radical paradigm shift, but not without strident reservations of the established core of conventional beekeepers who said, "Beekeeping is impossible without chemical intervention." Some added, "If you don't treat your bees, they'll die," in response to the push for treatment-free management.

Though some treatment-free beekeepers are showing a promising potential, the beloved, sage advice of the experienced, gray-haired, traditional beekeeper (translation: perceived wisdom), still feeds our anxiety. Can we really eliminate chemical treatments and not lose our bees?

Not to get off on a tangent, I think the answer is an enthusiastic, "Yes!"

But....

And you have to really listen because when anyone says one thing, then inserts a, "But..." they pretty much discount everything they said prior to the, "But..."

The conditions I might conjecture after my, "But..." would be to make sure you have good, resistant, hygienic behavior in your genetics. Too many beginners buy southern packages and expect them to instantly conform to treatment-free regimes. If you take chemically-dependent honey bees and callously withhold or remove their necessary medications, you get dead bees, not treatment-free bees, according to my esteemed colleague, Don Schram, from Michigan.

The second condition which seems to be the experience of many brave souls in the treatment-free community is the high, "wash-out," of susceptible colonies. Stories around the Internet and articles in some of the respected journals suggest a truly, treatment-free apiary has to endure two severe die-offs that purge the predisposed and vulnerable colonies. After two, massive cleansings, the population will then stabilize. But this scenario takes time, and patience. And in that time of transition, you'll sacrifice any ideals of abundant honey harvests.

The hard part is, of course, enduring the die-offs and rebuilding from the survivor colonies. I don't like die-offs, and frustrated beginners slink around the darkened corners of the auditoriums where I speak asking in whispered tones if treating a hive is really such a bad thing. I think the key component to treatment-free success is where you obtain your initial stock of bees before subjecting them to the rigors of no treatments.

Thankfully, some queen breeders and nuc producers are advertising their products as raised under treatment-free management.

Are treatments really necessary? Sadly, the fact remains that even treated bees are dying, and hence, with the concern for residues and resistance issues, the advent of organic ideals is rising like the dawn of a new day.

However, opponents to organic beekeeping proclaim those natural ideals are impractical, conceding our industry requires chemical intervention and always will, and thus organic production is impossible.

Impractical? Impossible? Really? How would anyone know if they haven't tried it? I have learned, no matter how solid my logic, I can expect some people to disagree, and disagree in varying degrees. But as much as the conventional beekeeping crowd advocates the recommended treatments, they don't have the survivorship to warrant or justify their methods. Treated bees are dying, but they will still insist on the necessity of treatments and argue vociferously against organic management or natural treatments. What gives?

It's been my pleasure to meet some of the most contrary people in life. That's sarcasm, if you didn't catch it. I find some people actually get a kick out of taking the opposing, divergent position. If you say the sky is blue, they'll argue that it is really clear, meaning, "colorless." They try and convince me the blue color of the sky detected by our eyes is technically a reflection of the vast ocean water. Technically, they are correct, yet my perspective is not necessarily false based on their truth, or their interpretation of how they apply that truth.

And, please, do not confuse them with the facts.

Then there are those people who can only see things one way which, of course, is <u>THEIR</u> way. We must always keep in mind what we perceive to be true is based on where we stand. Sometimes we need to take a different stand to see a different truth. Stand in a different place and you develop a different perspective, and sometimes all we need to do is turn around to gain that different perspective.

When the Wright brothers were trying to perfect the first airplane, they tried several different models. Some worked; some failed.

One day, they walked down to the sand dunes along the beach, carrying one of their experimental, model planes. Their neighbor approached them, walking along the same road. He thought the Wright brothers were wasting their time with their plans for flight.

"Hey, you Wright brothers," he called out. "You're wrong. You'll never get that thing to fly. If man were meant to fly, the good Lord would have given us wings! You don't know what you're doing."

The brothers paid no attention to the distracting banter. They continued down to the beach as if they didn't hear him. The neighbor turned and followed them down to the shoreline, taunting the brothers with his derision.

From the top of the dune, waiting for the right gust of ocean breeze, they launched the model into the wind. It glided down the beach for a considerable distance, beautifully and gracefully coming to rest gently as the wind slacked off. They turned to their harshly critical neighbor. Smiling broadly, they didn't say a word.

"Well, if you're going to do it THAT way, of course it's going to work," the neighbor conceded as he turned and walked away.

With every broadly generalized, universally applied statement of truth, there will always be an exception that falls outside the boundaries of concrete "truth." There is always an area of gray that causes one to stop and concede, "Well, yes but..." or "If you're going to do it THAT way."

One of my college professors was very sensitive to the ever-present, "Yes, but..." When a student asked a question, he would always pause to formulate his answer. Then he would frame and couch his response with the initial phrase, "With all things being equal..."

He knew that his answer would be shaded by a slight alteration in circumstances or a simple change of one variable. He knew there would always be an exception to what he was speaking as the truth. He also conceded, that in real life, things are never equal.

Sometimes he would begin his thoughtful response with the conditional phrase, "Well, based on what we know at the present..."

My professor was painfully aware that new knowledge comes to our awareness every day, and a new and innovative method is always right around the corner. provided I can train my dog to urinate on bee hives. New information presents itself and renders our certainty inept. Some discoveries shake the very foundation of our intelligence.

And even when this professor spoke an irrefutable answer known to be correct 99.99% of the time, the possibility existed for that .01% chance when someone did it <u>THAT</u> other way, his answer was incorrect or irrelevant. It really matters where one stands.

Moving Forward:

This is a book about organic beekeeping and how to apply organic management to a colony of honey bees, and how you might do it, THAT way. I wrote this book to address the interest from a growing segment in our apicultural community to raise bees, manage their hives and produce honey organically. If this is your desire, then let's get started.

However, I offer this caveat: If organic is something you see as impractical or impossible, something you adamantly oppose with every fiber of your being, just relax. You can set this book down and saunter on your merry way. I see no need to argue or debate. Your argument is not with me.

Neither is it my goal to make a passionate case for the superiority of organic beekeeping as the only way, or the best way, and begin a scurrilous diatribe against anyone who keeps bees in chemically-infused, vertically stacked, white boxes. I'd take exception to that statement, which has been aggressively ascribed to my apiaries, except most of my boxes are not white! They are colored with various shades of mistint paint, so I'm going to sidestep that criticism and conclude this charge does not apply to me!

Langstroth hives can be managed treatment-free or naturally, and are not indicative a chemically-addicted beekeeper.

But we also have to acknowledge there are chemical abuses in any industry, commercial beekeeping not excluded. However, the actions of what is likely a minority do not indict responsible beekeepers, even, "natural," beekeepers who happen to utilize Langstroth hives. Nor do such abuses on a commercial scale justify identifying alternative hive designs, such as the top bar hive, hex hive or Warre hive, as, "organic alternatives."

The revelations of industrial agriculture and chemically-enhanced food production, which implement commercial and migratory beekeeping for pollination, created tighter scrutiny of our standard apicultural practices, especially when the media took note of dying colonies. Some of these practices include the use of legally-registered miticides inside the hive and the supplemental feeding of high-fructose corn syrup.

The blowback, initiated by a host of environmentally-sensitive groups, spawned alternative ideologies in beekeeping. Several authors and promoters, with no working knowledge of what legally constitutes organic practices, promote their methodology as something like, "Natural beekeeping that keeps bees organically."

These apiaries are not, "organic," as we understand the definition of this word, which I'll clarify in a little bit.

Many of these well-intentioned, self-proclaimed, organic beekeepers are, "let-alone," beekeepers, who do not use artificial or synthetic drugs or supplemental feed, and operate according to the, "Bond," method (live and let die).   Other advocates refer to this as, "Tough Love Beekeeping."

While I have no personal beef with this style of management or these beekeepers, I see this method having nothing to do with organic principles, other than a philosophy that equates, "natural," with a benign neglect that allows the bees to sort out their problems without human interference or intervention.

And if you can make this method work, more power to you! But it does not fit the definition of organic, nor does, "natural," necessarily equate to, "organic."   And things that are truly organic, such as dog urine, are not necessarily helpful, healthful, effective or even necessary. Unless, of course, we start equating some random, anecdotal examples with a scientific methodology that also includes a control set which was left untreated.

These examples are but the tip of the iceberg calling for a common standard clarifying and defining exactly what constitutes organic production. Just because I call my operation, "organic," does not mean it is.   Just because I use, "natural," ingredients like hydrogenated vegetable and sugar patties does not fulfill what is legally defined as organic. It prevents someone like me from declaring my honey as an organic product just because I'm growing wild herbs in my garden and didn't put a chemical miticide in the colony.

Heaven knows there are multiple methods and a variety of management protocols in keeping honey bees.

The, "right," way to keep bees depends on your objectives and purposes, and how you measure success. Let your results speak for themselves and let the productivity and profitability of your colonies grade your management choices. After all, the bees are the best teachers, but they are also the harshest graders.

Always remember, "Beekeeping is local." What works in Missouri won't necessarily work in Montana, and what works in Montana may not translate to another beekeeper's management in Mississippi. There are organic principles and practices, but the management and methods will vary from region to region. Your results will challenge your desire to keep bees organically, and will test the limits of your resolve.

But be warned: should you choose to embark on an organic path, irrespective of what agricultural commodity you are producing, you'll enjoy and glean innumerous potential benefits, but the pitfalls will find every chink in your armor and challenge your boldest assumptions. You will experience dead bees and may feel frustrated to the point where you will be tempted to swing to the chemical side of beekeeping.

I hasten to encourage you to not give up too easily and choose a path of least resistance. Listen to your heart, but engage your brain. Remember and affirm the desires of why you entered beekeeping at such a challenging juncture in our present history. Be strong and of good courage. If this were easy, everyone would be keeping bees this way.

Beekeeping is an activity that is, "caught," more than it is, "taught." Keeping bees is like learning how to swim. I continue to believe that you can read all you want on how to swim, searching the Internet for lengthy blogs on the proper breathing and stroke techniques, but until you jump in over your head, you haven't really learned how to swim.

Beekeeping is like swimming. You either learn to swim or you sink. Many beginners, irrespective of their choice of utilizing either traditional chemical methods or natural management, soon quit. Perhaps the spirit is willing but the flesh is weak, perhaps beginners jump in where angels fear to tread, but the figure we toss around in the beekeeping circles is that 80% of all beginners, irrespective of which style of management they chose, will quit within two years.

Though I have yet to substantiate its validity, I find that statistic disheartening. Though not backed up with factual data, I find it anecdotally acceptable and probably pretty close to reality. As I ponder the whereabouts of people I've helped get started keeping bees, as I count the people missing from our local bee association meetings (and find myself running out of fingers), I begin to believe the statistic has merit.

The investment to get started is staggering, around $350 per hive, including bees, when you purchase new equipment. And when you lose your bees during the first winter, and you have to explain to your spouse or partner how replacement bees will cost another $100 to $150, and you still don't have any honey to show for your efforts, your hobby becomes an uphill battle and a source of constant tension every time it comes up in conversation.

But optimism still reigns over experience. Or maybe it's denial. It's like traveling down a road strewn with the wreckage of other drivers, watching numbed passengers stand on the shoulder where the vehicles lay stranded in the ditches, and we say, "But I still want to keep honey bees. I think I know how to make it work. I really believe this (_fill in the blank_) is the road to success."

As I speak at a number of conferences, I'm intrigued by the newcomers to beekeeping who pull me aside at meetings, speaking in hushed whispers, sharing with me the real secret to beekeeping success, which is, of course, "natural beekeeping." Little do they know, it's no secret, nor are they the first to attempt it, and it's not always successful. Braver newcomers have quit and gone home.

My suggestion, which has been echoed by other experienced beekeepers and teachers of beginning classes is this: 1) Find a local association, 2) Enroll in classes, 3) Hook up with a mentor, 4) Do everything the mentor says (even if they are "bent on chemicals"), and, 5) Once you get a couple of years under your belt and understand the basics of honey bee biology, start experimenting and expanding your apiaries to your organic or treatment-free ideals. You have to learn how to walk before you can run, and before you start walking, you'll begin by crawling.

There are many components to organic beekeeping. It is much more involved than simply eliminating chemicals or modifying the style of the hive, and it cannot merely be carried out with altruistic intentions, no matter how noble.

I take issue with beekeepers who intentionally ignore their bees and proclaim how they are, "All natural, baby!" Benign neglect may mimic bees in nature, but is far from the purposes carried out in organic management. It hardly qualifies as bee, "keeping," in my mind.

Which is why I put this little book together. It is my objective to peel back the implied simplicity and expound the intricate nature that enables honey bees to work together in harmony with their designed intentions and the environment in which they exist, and how we can do it organically.

My intent is to clarify how organic is defined, and how you might carry out your beekeeping management to call yourself an, "organic," beekeeper.

If you're ready, let's plow ahead.

Chapter 2:

What is, "Organic," Beekeeping,

and Why Bother?

My purpose in writing this book is to line out what it takes so you can make an informed decision to know what you have to do to comply with the principles of being organic. Yes, there are rules and definitions. Just because you sprinkle tea leaves across the front entrance of the hive does not give you the right to call yourself an organic beekeeper. And I don't care if you proudly proclaim how your bees have never looked better.

In order to give us a level playing field, and get us all on the same page, I will be using the organic protocols described by the United States Department of Agriculture, hence forth simply listed as the USDA. At times I'll refer to the National Organic Program as the NOP. The NOP defines the criteria for what constitutes organic production.

I presume the title of my book is self-explanatory of what you can expect in this manuscript. I also presume you picked up this book because you want to raise bees and produce honey organically, a desire I'll heartily commend.

However, if you want to earn my respect when you define and describe yourself as, "organic," let's agree to use the NOP standards and recommendations as the basis for that definition. I have little patience defining intentional neglect as something natural, and using common kitchen ingredients as opposed to synthetic chemicals will not necessarily qualify you as organic.

There will be substances all your beekeeping buddies use, some which might actually work, that will be prohibited under NOP organic protocols. These substances are clearly lined out on the, The National List, which defines what substances are allowed, and which are prohibited, to fulfill the organic definition.

The organic path will have costs and benefits, as well as advantages and disadvantages when compared to more conventional approaches to keeping bees. And, of course, conventional approaches have their own set of trade-offs, as well. I see both chemical and organic management as viable, especially when one can justify their chosen style of management as it fulfills their purpose for keeping honey bees.

I'm going to assume, since you are reading this book, your prevailing purpose is to maintain those clearly defined organic standards, above and beyond the aspiration of producing abundant honey harvests, and giving up the idealistic hope of keeping every hive alive, every year. Though it might border on the blasphemous, synthetic chemicals, when administered legally and responsibly, are weapons and tools to achieve the purpose of why we are keeping honey bees. I'll revisit this notion of purpose in a few pages.

I imagine you're willing to concede other conventional benchmarks in order to hold to the goals of your organic ideals. Under organic management, as it seems true under chemical management, you'll have hives die, and as I shared in the opening chapter, I hate losing a hive, for any reason, but most of all because of my incompetence, my procrastination, or my arrogance of choosing a so-called, natural method. I hate being forced to accept what could have been avoided. But then I come around and remember, if you're in the business of livestock, you have to get used to the reality of dead stock.

I also presume your philosophy of organic management will put the welfare of the bees as a higher priority than any commercial gain, and thus, you will weigh the merits and shortcomings of treating, or not. I will share, quite often, how my prevailing purpose for keeping honey bees is honey production.

Using the tools of IPM, I monitor my mite loads in order to make an informed decision on whether or not to treat, and what is the best treatment to handle the severity of the infestation. I contemplate the consequences of not treating. My heart's desire will always begin with the ideal of avoiding treatments, first and foremost, but if needed, to apply the least of the available evils.

When I speak of a, "noble intent," or a, "prevailing purpose," I'm talking about a general sense of possessing a ***vision***.

Vision is the ability to see beyond the immediate obstacles to see a finished product or reach a particular destination. In this case, your vision likely guides your management objectives to fulfill the definition of organic beekeeping, and how you produce healthy bees and maintain productive colonies organically. Do not underestimate the power of possessing a vision for what you want.

We unintentionally use our sense of vision every day. I may speak about a vacation to California that won't happen until next year. My vision guides me to make those preparations to secure a plane ticket and decide what I want to do when I arrive at Disneyland. When my vehicle breaks down and I'm forced to pirate my vacation budget to pay for the repairs, my vision helps me to find other ways to cut expenses and make my vacation possible.

When I open the kitchen cupboard and I see a bag of flour next to a can of hydrogenated vegetable oil, I can visualize a steamy batch of fresh-baked, chocolate chip cookies, even if I have yet to drive to the grocery store and purchase the chocolate chips. My vision of that end product motivates me to transcend the challenges of searching for my mother's favorite recipe, the one she used when we were young children. My vision is energized as I thirst for a glass of cold milk and hunger for the savory sweetness of those cookies before they have a chance to cool to room temperature. Vision is the quality that helps me see the task through to completion. Do not under-estimate the value of possessing vision.

If you want more information on vision and how it pertains specifically to beekeeping, I welcome you to take a look at one of my other resources, *"Sustainable Beekeeping: Surviving in An Age of CCD,"* available at https://www.createspace.com/4542110

In our culture, many people lack vision. Those who have it, initially, will become distracted by obstacles and challenges. They will lose sight of their goal. They give up or they compromise their vision by cutting corners or opting for the wide gate that leads to destruction. Our microwave society has no appreciation for hard work and we give in to the temptation to settle for too little. Nobody seems to have the patience to persevere for the long haul.

If you truly desire to keep bees organically, your vision will be the compass that directs your management decisions. It will be the Northstar in the evening sky that pulls you from some discouraging challenges and keeps you on the straight and narrow path to your intended destination.

The key is to remember your vision to keep bees organically, and keep that vision out in front of you to guide and inform your choices of your management options. Your vision will remind you why you chose to keep bees in this manner.

Three quotes, each whose origin escapes me as I've merely copied them down on scraps of paper and posted them to the dashboard of my truck, are as follows:

> "Everyone can rise above their circumstances and achieve success if they are dedicated to, and, passionate about, what they do."

> "The battle for the achievement of success is half won when one knows definitely what is wanted."

> "The secret of success in life is for a man to be ready for his opportunity when it comes."

The beekeepers whom I judge to be successful are those who know **_why_** they are keeping honey bees. Can you articulate why you want to keep bees, in general, and specifically, why you want to keep bees organically?

If you know the, "why," you'll discover the, "how." The beekeepers who know, "why," have a vision of what they want to accomplish, and their vision fuels their passion. Passion creates energy. But the key is having a vision, a goal as to why you are keeping bees, and in your case, keeping bees organically. That goal will direct your decisions in how you manage your bees, and sustain your fortitude to stay the course.

Sometimes people will challenge my zealous insistence why I compel people to explore and articulate the reasons why they want to keep bees, even if it isn't organically. Knowing why will focus your energy. Knowing why will clarify your management decision. Knowing why neutralizes the inherent distractions. Knowing why will steel your determination how you must do it this way, whatever way you decide.

Over the years, many people have approached me and requested help getting started keeping bees, and I'm all about helping others get started. Sadly, the vast majority of them were clueless as to why they wanted to keep bees.

A good portion of them, without a lick of experience, void of any knowledge, and lacking a preponderance of common sense, almost always mention something about, "natural," beekeeping, as if this method was the easiest way, gracefully paving the road to success for the inexperienced beekeeper.

It's as if we leave the bees alone they'll just figure everything out and we won't have to do any work. And I fully acknowledge my sense of feeling totally inadequate and completely overwhelmed every time I opened a bee hive in those early years. But good management has to learn what's happening in that stack of white boxes. Doing nothing may get you by, but it won't advance your expressed purpose for keeping bees.

Or, as one of my less-than-successful students complained, "I'm afraid to do anything because I might make a mistake, so I'd rather do nothing."

That lament rings true with me, reminding me of all the mistakes I've made over the years, some which decidedly accelerated the hive's demise. Yes, neglected colonies of bees might get by and survive all on their own, but they will not, normally, reward the bee keeper with any sweet compensation for sound, prudent management.

Again, I draw on the wisdom of my colleague, Don Schram, from Michigan, who said, "Management and stewardship is the difference. KEEPING bees is a responsibility. HAVING bees requires a credit card."

Desiring to keep a bunch of stinging insects in the back yard is something few rational people sign up for. So when approached about getting started, I typically inquire, in a friendly, non-adversarial way, "But why do you want to keep bees, and why now? It's such a challenging time keeping the bees alive. Beekeepers and bee hives are under tremendous pressure from pesticides and a mysterious disease we call, "Colony Collapse Disorder," or CCD. How do you think you'll find success when so many experienced beekeepers are falling by the wayside?"

Almost all of them ramble along with something vague, like, "Well, I've always been interested in bees. Bees are interesting and we want to raise our own honey so we can get back to eating more naturally, you know. And I've read how we need the bees. I have a garden to pollinate and I don't see as many bees as when I was a kid. And I'm hoping I can help to save the honey bee. We hear they're dying."

Well, okay, but that didn't really answer my question.

My follow-up question enlightens their real intent when I ask, "So what books have you read?"

This question raises a blank, deer-in-the-headlights stare, as if I was speaking a foreign language or asking a trick question. Sometimes they respond incredulously, with their own question, "There are books about beekeeping?"

That answer is self-explanatory. Yes, there are books. We've had them for hundreds of years. And you have to read them. I love the quote attributed to Mark Twain, which I've paraphrased, who said, "The beekeeper who can read and chooses not to, is no better off than the illiterate beekeeper who can't read."

Yes, by all means, get your hands on some books. I'd discourage any visits to your local library as their resources cater to a wider audience of the general public, but definitely peruse *www.amazon.com* and simply search for, "beekeeping." Yes, there are books. Kind of a novel idea, isn't it?

There are also a host of thousands of free videos on *www.youtube.com*, along with a million blog sites and an inexhaustible supply of "experts" who will render their opinions (and ignorance) on social media like Face Book or forums like *www.beesource.com.*

There is no excuse for failing to avail oneself to the information. However, folklore and anecdotal musings, along with plain stupidity, have replaced learned knowledge and factual evidence, especially on the Internet. You need to separate the wheat from the chaff. Still, the value of reading is to learn the jargon of beekeeping, and the language and vocabulary of beekeepers.

Without trying to appear like a wet blanket, in an attempt to clarify their thinking, I might push these potential beekeepers a little further and say, "But what is your purpose for keeping honey bees?"

Since most of my encounters take place at the farmer's markets, I think they see the commercial side of making a little money selling honey. Without any idea of how much work it takes to harvest, bottle and prepare my wares for the market, let alone get a honey crop from a hive, I fear I have made the process look too easy.

But making it look easy is the value of experience, and there are no short cuts to gaining experience.

Sometimes I mention a figure, in the neighborhood of $350 per hive, as what it costs to get started, and, of course, most beginning beekeeping courses suggest new beekeepers start out with two, even four hives, if they can afford it. This figure, "separates the men from the boys," identifying those who are vaguely interested and those who are resolutely committed to getting started.

Yeah, it's an expensive hobby. The cost figure usually brings up a discussion on acquiring used equipment in order to save money. Used equipment holds a remote potential for disease, and unless you really know what you're looking for, we generally recommend buying new equipment to get started. Once you see what the equipment looks like, many beginners try their hand at making their own from inexpensive, scrap lumber.

My journey into the upper levels of hive numbers meandered through the back roads of used equipment. In the days when I had more time than money, I scrounged old pallets and packing crates and made my own boxes. If you want the whole story, with all the gritty details, I go into detail in my book, *"Beekeeping with Twenty-five Hives,"* which can be purchased at,

https://www.createspace.com/4152725

I'm not saying it can't be done, but there are easier ways to get started than by searching for used equipment.

Despite the high attrition rate of beginners, many of them are holding on to their equipment to give it another go at a later date, like when they have that extra $150 to buy another nuc.

It doesn't surprise me when the majority of these potential beekeepers respond with, "I'll get back to you." And, of course, they never do. There are also a million potential beekeepers who are waiting for, "someday," as in, "Someday when I'm not so busy," or, "Someday when we move to the country."

Many new beekeepers without vision give it a pretty good try, but after their first year, the bees die. But they've hung on their boxes in the hopes that, "someday," they'll get back into bees. Okay, whatever.

I'm going to strongly suggest you steep your vision with solid commitment, not just a passing interest. When I hear of people committing themselves to disciplined investment strategies in the stock market and making good profits, I often hear other people say, "I'd sure like a little extra money to play the market."

To those who are committed to the application of sound investment principles, there is no such thing as, "playing," the market. Your investment in beekeeping should be as solidly committed and disciplined.

I think the first step in keeping bees organically is to take a stand, that is, to make your proclamation (even if it just to yourself) that you are going to be an organic beekeeper. Let this be your prevailing purpose, your vision. Drive a corner post in the ground. Stake your claim that this is what you want to do; this is where you want to go. Be prepared for the conventional beekeepers in your local association, the ones, "bent on promoting chemicals," to tell you how it's impossible; how it's impractical; how all your bees are going to die.

Rather than argue, just smile and say, "Then I want to be *as organic as possible*." This statement will cause some to politely smirk, and those within earshot may roll their eyes at you behind your back. Don't worry about convincing them. Focus on your resolve. I promise you, any attempt to debate your detractors will be pointless, fruitless and futile. You'll have better success if you wander outside and argue with a fresh, steamy pile of dog droppings. But maybe you can find an innovative new mite treatment, so all is not lost!

Or you can ignore my advice, pick up your battle shield and take them on, but don't count on many converts. There's an old expression about wrestling with a pig. You both get muddy and the pig kind of enjoys it. Not that conventional beekeepers are pigs, mind you, but some who have years of success with traditional beekeeping management will enjoy a good debate with you on the folly of your organic ideals. Let your success make your argument for you.

The good news is there are many different ways to keep honey bees, and countless ways to produce honey. There are tricks and tips for every methodology. Every way has some upside as well as a downside, advantages as well as disadvantages. We'd all be better off if we just respected each other's opinions, and ignorance, and went about our own business of raising honey bees.

But beyond just declaring your intent to produce honey organically, ponder the, "why." What motivates you to keep honey bees in this manner? What drives your passion to follow organic protocols? Is there a reason why you want to specialize and raise honey bees organically, or even just, "more naturally," even if it is _as organically,_ or _as naturally, as possible_?

I started out keeping bees in 1981 when the environment was friendlier to the honey bees. We had much more floral diversity and less monoculture (single crops monopolizing the fields from horizon to horizon). My intent was to raise my bees organically, but the definition of what constituted, "organic," was extremely unclear, vague and left up to a producer's opinion or ignorance.

Second, life, in general, and beekeeping, more specifically, was simpler, more innocent, and did not require extreme measures of antibiotics and synthetic miticides. To be a beekeeper, you simply tossed a package of bees in a box, then you got out of their way as they made monster crops of honey with very little intervention on our part.

Then life got more complicated with environmental pollution, the destruction of fence-row habitats, the introduction of non-selective herbicides (read: Roundup®), and an increased pressure to coax every last bushel of production from every square inch of farmland. Farming was a precarious game of decreasing margins, and most of our industrial food production was driven, more and more, by chemical inputs. Monoculture squeezed out the beneficial rotation of crops and a floral diversity.

Then in the mid-1980s, the varroa mite started spreading. Chemical intervention, at the time our best weapon against hive mortality, was seen as the answer. And it worked, for a while. Little did we know the mites would develop resistance to these chemicals. Residues from some of these legally approved, supposedly, "safe," miticides were taking up residence in our wax comb. The notion that we should be concerned was not on our radar.

We had not yet discovered how these residues affect the long-term health of the colony. We found ourselves scrambling for bigger, better weapons in a very small, under-developed and dwindling arsenal. Others began experimenting with, "kitchen sink," concoctions and herbal recipes. They talked up the bee clubs and pronounced, "My bees have never looked better."

So I started to make adjustments, as well, looking more to, "natural," treatments rather than buying into the conventional, chemical responses to our problems. My option of choice remains an organic fumigant, formic acid, which is still shunned by some beekeepers as a, "chemical," treatment. Trust me, it's organic and it's on the approved list according the National Organic Program.

My adjustments and revisions with natural treatments for mites catered to my purpose for keeping bees, which was honey production. My success with natural treatments, however, was hit and miss.

Even though I liked the idea of being organic, which at this time had not been defined by the NOP, I was only interested, not committed. I hated losing a colony of bees to what was seen, at that time, as a preventable problem thanks to chemical intervention.

I shared my dilemma with the experts. Their question, in response, became, "Why let a colony die when you can keep it alive with an easily administered chemical treatment that's safe and convenient?"

I have to confess, it sure made sense to me. But the effectiveness of the chemicals was waning, while the costs were increasing. Safety and convenience always seemed paradoxical in my mind.

My prevailing purpose for keeping bees when I started remains today, namely, to manage my bees to be healthy and productive, to manage them with intensive goals to maximize my potential honey harvest, then to extract and market that honey on a retail level. Translation: I'm in it for the money, and I'm not opposed to using chemicals to achieve those ends, but chemicals will be my last option.

There are many, "soft," and, "natural," options at my disposal before I reach the chemical end of the spectrum.

So, yes. I'm in it for the money. Usually, I'm not quite so forthcoming. Anytime I've mentioned how I manage my colonies with the idea of harvesting an abundant honey crop, I usually get a back-handed retort of, "Well, we're not going to be in it for the money," implying, "at least, not like you, Grant."

And that's fine. I keep bees with the primary philosophy of a commercial beekeeper, to utilize the bees' natural instincts and their proclivity to gather nectar and store honey. I work **with** the bees, and in a certain regard, they work **for** me, but it is more of a collaboration of preparation and diligence, along with some breaks in the weather.

And I get a kick out of someone who feels compelled to remind me, a pastor, that the Good Book warns that, "money is the root of all evil," a mistranslation of what more correctly admonishes, "the <u>LOVE</u> of money is a root of all kinds of evil."

Actually, I think it's the <u>LACK</u> of money that is the root of all this evil, but I digress. What I'm after here is for you to clarify your thinking as to why you want to raise honey bees, and if your purpose is to raise them organically, then I want you to be honest with yourself as to why you want to go down this very specific road. And buckle up. It's going to be a bumpy ride.

I like the idea of organic management, even ideals of treatment-free beekeeping. But I need living colonies of healthy bees. I am not averse to using chemicals as a weapon of last resort.

Bear in mind, with my goals and purposes, I always kept the collateral damage from chemicals in the forefront of my management practices. I will always gravitate to something more natural or mechanical as my first option.

While not exactly and precisely, "organic," I want a treatment that is safe and effective to help my bees maintain a reasonable level of health. I embrace a quasi-Hippocratic oath, so to speak, that any treatment I subject my bees to, should first, "do no harm." I think organic management is the best option to do no harm. But my ultimate purpose is to produce honey.

And again, I presume by picking up this book, your purpose for keeping honey bees is to keep them organically, or like the young lady I introduced in the first chapter, your vision is to raise bees and produce honey, _as organically as possible_. So let's move from your intent to keep bees organically to some of the obstacles to this declaration as you stake your apicultural claim.

As I lay out what it takes to keep bees organically, I will stress that this notion of, "organic," is not to be taken lightly. I'm going to describe what it takes, "according to the book." The book, in this case, is the National Organic Program and their standards and recommendations that demand compliance in order to earn the descriptive word, "organic," to our production and marketing. But this was not always so.

Many years ago, several vendors at the farmer's markets posted signs above their produce advertising, "Organic Beets," "Organic Lettuce," or whatever they wanted to market under this description.

If asked what they meant by, "organic," they might generically suggest how they didn't use any pesticides to spray the crop. Or perhaps they used a, "natural," biological insecticide like Bacillus thuringiensis, sometimes noted as, "Bt." Or maybe they followed the advice of Jerry Baker, "America's Master Gardener," who pioneered any number of the so-called, "natural remedies," back-to-basic tonics and environmentally-friendly antidotes comprised of Listerine® antiseptic mouthwash, Epsom salts, baby shampoo, beer and garlic.

And while these tonics may work (or not), nothing about them was specifically, "organic." Have you ever read the ingredient label on a bottle of baby shampoo?

C'mon, man!

While these so-called, supposedly organic farmers were marketing their crops, they had no real standards to consistently follow that would validate these crops as organic. Consumers had no measure of accountability to hold over their organic management. Even if nothing was topically applied to the crops, these farmers may have used a commercial, synthetic fertilizer and a chemical herbicide. Or they may have been organic in their production for this particular year, but the soil was polluted with chemical residues from last year's crop. The crop may have been irrigated with chemically treated water from a municipality, or from a stream containing runoff from a chemically treated farm.

In too many places and circumstances, the definition of this word, "organic," took on too many nuances and opinions, many based on folk-lore or old wives' tales (like human hair to scare away deer or blood-meal from a slaughter plant to discourage rabbits). When I gardened and sought to do so organically, I liked the idea of using blood meal (for what, I can't remember), but I did not examine where the blood came from, or what antibiotics were fed to the livestock that may still be present in that blood. I just accepted the notion that if it came from a living animal, it just had to be organic.

The whole realm of what qualified as organic had no boundaries, no limitations, no rules and no parameters. If I said I was organic, people had to take me at my word. But in reality, the organic industry had no integrity. My produce was organic because I said it was organic.

Some produce marketed as, "organic," was anything but, and may have been horticulturally blessed by a host of undisclosed, synthetic chemicals to grow a nice, picture-perfect, consumer-appealing fruit, which is nothing short of deceptive marketing tactics. But when you looked at that vendor at the farmer's market, in his dirt-stained overalls and tattered straw hat, you couldn't help but believe the merchandise before you was honestly organic. And maybe it was, but you didn't know for sure. The reliability of the organic movement was compromised. Any producer could put up a sign saying anything.

That's when our federal government, under the auspices of the USDA, restricted the use of the descriptive label, "organic," to *certified* producers, which meant anybody using that word had to prove their produce was organic, by the NOP definition, and further, they had to have a third party verify the accuracy and certify their records.

These third-parties had to know the requirements, themselves, in order to hold the organic production accountable to the NOP's definition. You were not allowed to reach into your garden shed and pull out an old, crumpled seed packet with some random notes scribbled on it, or wipe the sweat from your brow as you squint into the sunset and tell the certifying agent you never used chemicals in fifteen years.

The organic movement really took shape with the Organic Foods Production Act of 1990, enacted under the 1990 farm bill, which authorized a National Organic Program (NOP) to be administered by the USDA through the Agricultural Marketing Service (AMS). With this legislation, the push for legitimate organic standards began.

But, like most of our government programs, it would not happen over night. It stumbled out of the gate due to a lack of funding. It would be ten years, in 2000, before the final rules were drawn out and defined, allowable practices clarified, and the list of specific prohibited and allowed inputs finalized, what we now have as the National List.

This is when the organic movement became a viable force. The Organic Foods Production Act act restricts the use of the word, "organic," **only** to those producers who willingly comply with the rules, submit records of production, and offer their records to be inspected and certified as accurate.

In an effort to curtail the shenanigans of the chemical charlatans and snail-oil gardeners, the USDA established and implemented the NOP and defined what it means to be an organic producer. The NOP requirements are not mere suggestions or best management practices as to how to produce organic crops, produce and livestock. They are mandates.

Anyone using the word, "organic," must 1) prove they were, indeed, following the stringent rules and precise requirements for a set period of time prior to calling the produce, "organic," 2) keep excruciatingly detailed records, and 3) make those records available for inspection and certification.

But missing from the Organic Foods Production Act was clear rules for honey bees and organic honey production. An NOSB Apicultural Task Force was charged to develop the apicultural standards. In September of 2001, a draft was released, and it was later finalized in October of 2010.

If you're a beekeeper, you know between 2001 and 2010 great adversities challenged the livelihood of beekeepers and bulldozed the topography of apicultural landscape. In 2006, Colony Collapse Disorder was defined. Varroa mites continued their rampage and Small Hive Beetles moved across the country. Africanized Honey Bees kept advancing northward. The task force came out with recommendations with the admission beekeeping was still in a state of flux.

However, these recommendations have not yet become law. They are still just recommendations. They are still under review. Basically, we have no apicultural standards for organic beekeeping. There is nothing to enforce; there is nothing to hold anyone accountable. There are no rules by which anyone can be certified, at least for producing organic honey.

When the discussion of organic standards rises at the farmer's markets, I hear nothing but frustration from the majority of vendors. They complain how the government has made it impossible to produce any crop organically, as if the government was trying to eliminate any and all organic food.

Those who sought certification have found the organic process tedious and expensive. In some instances, it is impossible to find a knowledgeable person to certify their records. Once found, the cost is prohibitive.

Despite such conspiratorial cynicism, my manuscript intends to promote a strict definition of what constitutes organic, as lined out by the NOP, even though these rules and regulations have languished as mere recommendations and have yet to become officially sanctioned. I'm going to treat them as law. The NOP standards will be that common ground by which we can agree before we start debating if human ear wax is, indeed, an organic method to control fruit flies in a bowl of bananas.

If it is your desire to produce honey organically, such that you can call yourself, "organic," there will be definite protocols to avoid and many which you are not allowed to use, **PERIOD**. With deep respect to Mr. Jerry Baker and the volumes of anecdotal evidence suggesting those tonics work like magic, they may not bear the name, "organic."

SPOILER ALERT: Guess what? The organic protocols for organic beekeeping in the United States are next to impossible to satisfy, which I will explain as we move along into subsequent chapters.

Still, do not let me deter your desire to keep honey bees organically. I will detail the requirements, and in some cases, you will find insights into how you can manage your bees organically, or *as organically as possible*, even if you never hope to pursue a certification.

Obviously, if compliance to the standards is impossible, then certification is equally impracticable, unattainable, unachievable, and completely out of the question. Still, I will present the NOP standards as if certification was the goal.

That said, you can still satisfy your own conscience that you are doing your bees a favor by following, *as much as possible*, the organic protocols. You might be able to keep some, but I can almost guarantee you won't be able to have your all your management decisions and every apiary location certified as organic.

But is certification your purpose in keeping bees organically, or is it your desire to satisfy your own criteria that your management is *as organic as possible*? The reality is you will have to ratchet your aspirations higher if you ever hoped to have that nice, green and white logo on your label. Or move to some foreign country where the organic standards are lower.

But let's return to your purpose, your intent, your vision in keeping bees organically. Is it your desire to put up with the certification process, or are you doing this for your own peace of mind and the welfare of your bees?

I hasten to guess that 99% of today's beekeepers seeking organic status merely want to sleep at night, believing they are doing the best job they can by raising their bees as naturally as possible, to the best of their abilities. They want to look their customers in the eye and state with confidence and integrity that they have a pure product. They've done their best to protect the bees from harmful pesticides. But they will not be able to call their product, "organic."

And this is where I'm going to be a fuss budget, a legalistic pharisee, a nit-picker, a royal P.I.A. when it comes to people who say, "Oh yeah, I'm organic because I'm all natural."

Stop. If you have no standards as to what constitutes organic beekeeping, then I'm going to insist you respect me as part of the Royal Family of England because I once watched five minutes of Princess Diana's wedding.

The idea that organic can mean anything you want is the very reason the Organic Food Production Act was warranted. Ignorance, arrogance and this self-righteous attitude of deciding what's organic and what's not is the reason the organic movement lost all credibility. Let's get on the same page and bring some integrity to the name, "organic." It cannot go back to meaning whatever I want it to mean, given my laziness and lack of accountability.

Again, that said, I'm going to line out the NOP requirements, which at this point are mere recommendations. I confess, because of the locations where I keep my bees, I will never be certified. I cannot make the grade. My apiary locations are surrounded by conventional, chemical agriculture.

Additionally, because my purpose in keeping bees is for honey production, albeit as naturally as possible, I am not opposed to using a non-organic or unapproved intervention to save the life of my colonies. And by using the term, "unapproved," I mean a treatment that is still legally registered and approved by the EPA, though it may not satisfy the organic standards as set forth by the NOP.

By the way, powdered sugar, a safe, largely innocuous food product is mildly effective for treating a hive for varroa mites. However, if you shift the use of a food product to address a parasitic mite issue, you have changed the technical nature of powdered sugar to a pesticide, and powdered sugar is not approved by our government as a registered pesticide for varroa mites.

Yes. Really. It's the same stuff, but when you change the purpose of the application, you have to conform your actions to a different set of governmental regulations. It's crazy, but it's our legal system. Learn to live with it.

The same goes for oxalic acid, commonly sold in every hardware store in America. It's an organic wood bleach used by furniture refinishers. It's also an effective drench when dribbled on a cluster of honey bees in their broodless cluster in the winter. So as I mix oxalic acid in a 10% sugar solution, and an inspector shows up as I'm dribbling the drench between the frames and over the cluster, I'll have to say, "Golly, officer, I'm just bleaching my top bars to make them look pretty."

Yep. Same stuff, different application, and I'm in violation of United States law despite the fact that oxalic acid is legally available as an organic pesticide in Canada.

Go figure.

Herein lies some of the most ironic, bureaucratic stupidities of our government. As it pertains to organic beekeeping, the USDA has recommendations that have not yet been approved. Because these recommendations have not yet been formally approved or sanctioned, there are no formal, organic rules to govern beekeeping, and no rules by which you can have your apiary deemed, "organic."

There are no official organic standards. The recommendations are still nothing but recommendations. Because there are no rules, there is nothing to authoritatively certify any beekeeping operation as legitimately organic in the United States.

Because the agencies that could certify your honey lack any approved, clearly defined, governmental regulations, they have no guidance as to what legally constitutes the standards for organic honey.

Therefore, until the certifying agents have approved regulations, they can only shrug and say they have nothing to base their certification on.

As a default, until the government adopts the recommendations as law, beekeepers are urged to work with a certifying agent and fall back on the general regulations for, "livestock," which have been approved.

But honey bees don't quite fit that classification as livestock. Well, too bad. At this time, this is your option.

From the Organic Apicultural Recommendations:

"In the interim, certifiers have used the existing Livestock Standards as a baseline for certifying organic apiculture operations, Sections 205.236 to 205.239, and the related sections of the National List, Sections 205.603 and 205.604. The fact that apiculture varies considerably from other livestock operations has lead to a great deal of variability in the requirements of certification. Growing pressure from the apiculture industry, the certifier community and the movement toward equivalency agreements spawned a renewed effort to develop apiculture specific organic standards."

But we're still waiting for these recommendations to become official standards. It's like a, "catch-22." You can't be approved for following the rules because the rules have not been defined, only suggested. And because you are not approved or certified, you are prohibited from using the term, "organic," on your honey label.

And again, I hearken to the organic ideals in these recommendations. Just because our government fiddles and farts, postulates and gesticulates over tedious minutiae is no excuse not to follow your dreams and live your passion to keep bees organically. If you are not keeping bees organically for certification, do it for the welfare of your bees. Follow the recommendations so you sleep at night knowing you've taken the road less traveled.

But do not think you can use the term, "organic," anywhere or anytime. This is law, even though the law won't ever let you use the word. This is part of that conspiratorial cynicism I mentioned earlier. You'll just have to take the higher road.

So though not formally sanctioned, I'm still going to use these recommendations as if they were approved, because some day they will be approved.

Well, okay. Maybe. Hopefully.

My interest in keeping bees *as organically as possible*, or *as chemical-free as possible*, even *as naturally as possible* stems from many challenges. Pests and parasites have developed resistance to legally-registered, synthetic pesticides, the ones approved for in-the-hive use. I'm concerned about chemical residues in wax honey comb migrating to the honey. I'm concerned about the side effects from supposedly, "safe," chemicals that alter a honey bee's ability to fend off viruses, an area we call, "epigenetics."

It's hard to imagine that something used to kill a parasitic mite may be making my bees susceptible to viruses, that synthetic chemicals might be compromising their immune system, actually making them sick and vulnerable to bacterial infections.

No. Wait. It's not that hard!

I want to market a wholesome product, unadulterated (no matter how unintentional) and free of chemicals. I want to confidently market a pure product that I can stand behind, something I put my name on and be proud. I want to eat my own honey and know that it is safe!

Now that's a tall order! Going organic is not easy, and as we move along in this book, I'll show you how challenging it is to be organic. There will be compromises to your hopes to produce a profitable honey crop and keep your bees alive.

As much as I strive to keep my hives chemical-free, _as organic as possible_, I'm still surrounded by agricultural interests that utilize prohibited chemicals to produce their respective crops. These are factors outside the realm of my control but they have a huge impact on my ability to keep bees, and keep bees alive! But I can still hold on to my vision to manage the hives organically, even as I face anti-organic environmental problems!

You may also find yourself facing a preventable problem in the hive that requires some kind of intervention not allowed in the organic requirements. As for me and my house, I like to keep bees alive, and if the problem is preventable, I will sacrifice my organic ideals to keep bees alive and utilize the legally-approved resources.

This goes back to my personal, prevailing purpose of producing honey, which is why I used that idea as the lead topic for this chapter. I need living bees to produce honey. I need healthy bees and a prolific queen to raise an army of foragers. Dead bees are lousy honey producers, and I should know as I've tried it over several seasons. :)

Other beekeepers may choose to sacrifice a failing colony to keep their commitment to being organic. Which is fine if being organic is your prevailing purpose. However, the organic standards do not allow a beekeeper to sit back and allow a preventable problem to kill a hive. Organic standards focus on sustainable practices and conservation of resources. You simply have to find a way to address the situation from an organic standpoint.

Or in my case, I may opt for a chemical response. However, in the organic scheme of things, any chemical intervention will prevent me from legitimately using the word, "organic." I may have to compromise and describe my practices, *as organic as possible*.

I've seen a number of vendors at several markets post signs that read, "Non-certified Organic," when describing their management practices. This suggests they follow organic protocols, to the best of their ability, but for some reason have not sought the validation of their practices to become certified. Maybe they are organic, in theory, but since it is impossible to comply to the standards, in practice, the choose to fudge the compliance.

Maybe they are organic. Maybe they follow the standards and those standards for their operation have been approved as law. But getting certified is expensive. I have a hunch they have chosen the path of least resistance (stating they are, "non-certified") due to the cost and the hassle of record keeping and accountability.

I also ponder the possibility that the practices they consider organic may not, necessarily, follow the recommendations of the NOP. In this case, they are cheating. And if the government was trying to cut out all the fakery and forgery of legitimately defined organic practices, it doesn't seem to be working. Someone found a loop-hole.

Further, unless you are legitimately certified, you are prohibited from using the word, "organic," on your label. The fine for such an offense is $11,000, but then who is checking? Where does the enforcement lie, other than market managers who should know the rules and the restrictions on calling anything organic, unless it is certified.

I'm not aware of any rules or exemptions granting permission declaring how one can be, "non-certified," which seems to be an admission of guilt and failure to follow the law. But to use that wording, in my opinion, means you know what it takes to be, "organic," and you have full knowledge that you are supposed to be, "certified," but you choose not to, even if such certification is impossible.

So here are producers are using the word, "organic," even if it is, "non-certified," which represents an attractive angle to consumers who really have little knowledge of what it takes to be organic, but they know it's something good. These consumers may have no clue what it means to be certified, or what certified means. All they see is the word, "organic," and they are lulled into a state of trusting the producer.

And I'm intrigued by the vendors who have a home-made, hand-written sign with, "ORGANIC," spelled out in large letters, and above it in a font one-fourth the size, "non-certified."

Hmmmm. Is that really kosher?

Okay, Grant. Get off the soap box. Get back to your purpose. My prevailing purpose in this book is to share with you how to produce organic honey and raise bees organically, as I understand the NOP protocols. And again, I will confess I do not produce organic honey that fulfills the strict certification requirements.

In reality, I can't be organic, raise my bees organically, or produce organic honey, even if I knew of someone who could certify my apiaries, even if the recommendations became legal regulations and organic standards. I don't profess or advertise my honey as organic, nor do I put that word on my labels. I can't. It's the law.

And I'm not going to participate in the, "non-certified," monkey business. Even with that disclaimer, I am still obligated to follow the NOP standards for organic apiculture.

Nevertheless, I know how to do it, what it takes and how it can be done. But there are losses and gains, costs and benefits to organic apiculture. It's up to you to decide if you are committed to producing organic honey for your own personal pride and conscience, or if you, like me, are committed to another goal in beekeeping that may force you to forfeit a legitimate organic label though you strive to be *as organic as possible*.

However, there are two, "wild cards," to this cavernous labyrinth of government regulation. <u>First</u>, if your gross income from organic production is $5,000 or less per year, you can claim an exemption from being certified. It does not release you from maintaining the strict requirements for organic production, it just means, if you follow them, you can be your own source of self-accountability. But you still need to handle your honey according to the handling requirements, and you still need to maintain verifiable records.

<u>Second</u>, if you should find someone who can certify your operation as organic, they have the option of using the existing Livestock Standards as a baseline, with certain variables from the approved/prohibited list that applies to apiculture, found in Sections 205.236 through 205.239, and 205.603 through 205.604.

Until the apicultural standards and recommendations become sanctioned regulations, there is a little bit of, "wiggle room," open to a little interpretation and equivalency, that may be used in the interim. Hopefully, someday, the apicultural standards will be approved and this, "gray area," cleared up to a definitive, "black and white."

Additionally, until the NOP develops clear standards, accredited certifiers have the option of using European and Canadian standards to harmonize a workable solution, but this remains the discretion of the accredited certifier. These variables keep the ideals of organic honey production inconsistent, and certifiers are given a little, "wiggle room," to negotiate the standards. This may give you some alternatives to your frustrations with the USDA protocols.

Maybe.

If you want to try and skate by on not using the word, "organic," but try and use the word, "natural," the USDA still has a vested interest in how people and producers use and interpret this word. As required by the USDA, meat, poultry and egg products labeled as, "natural," must be minimally processed and contain no artificial ingredients.

The descriptive term, "natural," has no bearing on any standards regarding farm practices or management. It only applies to the processing of meat and egg products. If your product (i.e., honey) does not contain meat or eggs, there are no standards for using this adjective.

In my opinion, the number one problem with keeping a colony of honey bees healthy is the varroa mite. Infestations of varroa mites will take down a colony of bees over the course of a season. We have effective chemicals to combat varroa mites, as well as some, "natural," applications of soft chemicals (more on this later). But even some of the so-called, natural approaches do not fit the organic criteria.

Since my purpose is to produce honey, I need to keep bees alive. I monitor mite levels and will address the infestation as naturally, as unobtrusively as possible. I highly prefer natural and organic approaches, but if the infestation warrants a chemical application in order to save the colony, I will acquiesce and apply the chemical responsibly.

I've tried to be organic and follow the rules, but my hive losses were too high. Some people will tell me I'm weeding out the susceptible colonies and killing off the inferior bees with my natural selection. But that's not my purpose. I produce honey. I need bees.

It gets back to what my purpose is, and what your purpose might be as well. If your purpose is to raise bees organically, you will have losses. These losses may have been prevented with chemical intervention, but your purpose was to be organic and thus you will have to accept a certain level of otherwise preventable loss.

Many of my colleagues in the St. Louis area are ardent, treatment-free beekeepers. While not strictly, "organic," as there are many layers and aspects to following the rules and regulations to be a certified, organic beekeeper, they refuse to interject chemicals into their hives. They shrug and suggest their losses are part of the treatment-free program and they hope someday to weed out the susceptible bees and breed queens from the survivors.

I lend my support to my treatment-free colleagues and wish them the best of luck. They are following their purpose. Though they have losses, they are to be commended for their unwavering dedication to, and discipline of their purpose.

The applied lesson of this chapter is to define why you want to keep honey bees, and specifically, why you want to go the route of organic management. The better you know your reasons, the more clarified your vision becomes.

Do not underestimate the power of vision. To know the, "why," will unleash the, "how."

Chapter 3:

What does it mean to be, "Organic?"

What is organic?

Organic is a labeling term that indicates that the food or other agricultural product has been produced through approved methods that integrate cultural, biological, and mechanical practices that foster cycling of resources, promote ecological balance, and conserve biodiversity. Synthetic fertilizers, sewage sludge, irradiation, and genetic engineering may not be used.

How Are Organic Products Overseen?

The National Organic Program regulates all organic crops, livestock, and agricultural products certified to the United States Department of Agriculture (USDA) organic standards. Organic certification agencies inspect and verify that organic farmers, ranchers, distributors, processors, and traders are complying with the USDA organic regulations.

USDA conducts audits and ensures that the more than 90 organic certification agencies operating around the world are properly certifying organic products. In addition, USDA conducts investigations and conducts enforcement activities to ensure all products labeled as organic meet the USDA organic regulations.

The USDA organic regulations describe the specific standards that farmers and processors must meet to use the word, "organic," or the USDA seal on food, feed or fiber.

Consumers purchase organic products expecting that they maintain their organic integrity from farm to market. Through enforcement, USDA creates a level playing field by taking action against farmers and businesses that violate the law and jeopardize consumer confidence in organic products. Overall, organic operations must demonstrate that they are protecting natural resources, conserving biodiversity, and using only approved substances.

In order to sell, label, or represent their products as organic, operations must follow all of the specifications set out by the USDA organic regulations. And according to Section 205.101, anyone using the word, "organic," must be certified and must meet all the requirements.

Organic certification verifies that your farm complies with the USDA organic regulation and allows you to sell, label, and represent your products as organic. These regulations describe the specific standards required for you to use the word, "organic," or the USDA organic seal.

Okay. You're going to make the commitment to be organic. That's the good news. The bad news is, if you intend to call yourself an, "organic beekeeper," or use the adjective, "organic," to describe your operation, your management, your apicultural products (honey, pollen, propolis, royal jelly, beeswax and bee venom), or sell and market them as, "organic," then you must follow all the regulations, and develop a written Organic Systems Plan (OSP) to show how you will follow all the regulations.

The OSP is the first part. It is the written plan that includes all your management decisions, which approved inputs you'll use and where you will acquire them, how you're going to monitor your hives, the frequency of the applications, how you're going to handle the harvest and storage, in addition to how you're going to keep records and verify the plan is effectively implemented.

This in accordance with Section 205.201 (and I don't know about you, but I'm exhausted already). Writing and OSP should be easy as you already have a vision. Write your OSP like a business plan. Articulate your vision like a mission statement.

Record keeping will be a huge part of your organic production, and your OSP needs to address how you will keep the required records. If you are not completely organic, or have some apiaries under organic production and others that are not, you have what the NOP refers to as a, "split," operation. Your records must reflect what you do in each apiary, and you must describe the management practices you use to keep the hive products from co-mingling and contamination, which may result from bee drift or robbing.

A producer of organic apiculture products must maintain records in accordance with Section 205.103 and Section 205.236(c). Split operations are required to identify hives that have been treated with materials not permitted under Section 205.603 or materials prohibited under Section 205.604.

Records must include:

(1) map of the forage zone, the surveillance zone, and the flowering times of the various plants in those zones for all bee yards

(2) affidavits verifying the 3 year land management history for the certified forage zones

(3) sources of foundation and whether foundation is organic

(4) date of last use of prohibited substances

(5) identification system for hives and bee yards

(6) verification that all comb has been drawn out under organic management

(7) the season these "clean" frames had been used for the production of organic honey

(8) a system of tracking hives, queens introduced or raised, monitoring through the season

(9) a list of inputs used and labels of inputs

(10) records of feeding including materials and dates

(11) source of any organic sugar, organic honey, organic pollen and/or organic pollen substitutes fed to colonies; certification documentation for materials fed
(12) records of all health care interventions and products used
(13) estimated yields of all bee products per hive
(14) dates of harvest of bee products
(15) sales records of bee products
(16) packaging and labeling for bee products sold

The second part, after writing the OSP, is to have your OSP approved and certified by an accredited agency. Actually, I think it's a grand idea to develop your OSP in consultation with a certifier so you start out on the same page, literally and figuratively. Finding one is not as easy as you might think, especially for apiculture, and the process is not cheap. Sources vary, but I've heard certifications costs for other commodities running from $5,000 upwards to $20,000.

This does not sound like something I can afford. Here's some good news: if you market less than $5,000 in gross sales of your apicultural products, you're exempt from being certified. Further, if you market less than $5,000 in gross sales, you do not have to write out an OSP and it does not have to be approved by the certifying agency.

But you still have to follow all the rules of production and handling your products according to the organic regulations.

So now I'm confused. If I sell less than $5,000 worth of product, I can call my operation, "organic," provided I adhere to all the regulations. But how do I know what those regulations are, and how does anyone else know that I kept them? The value of the OSP assures me, and my customers, that I know what I'm doing!

If someone, like a potential customer asked you, "How do you manage your bees organically, and how do I know this honey is organic?"

Do you know how to answer that question?

An OSP, while a lot of work, is empowering. Write it. Don't be lazy.

And just how much is $5,000 worth of gross sales? As an example, we sell our honey (non-organic, not certified) for $14 a quart. It takes 358 quarts to reach $5,000, and if I guess that an average super will give me about ten quarts of honey (very roughly calculated), then 36 supers should reach this $5,000 gross retail total.

If, in my area, I can guess and expect (and hope and dream, in some years) that an average hive will produce about two supers per hive, then I can probably slide by with the production from eighteen hives and not worry about writing an OSP or paying a certifying agent.

So I can use the word, "organic," provided I've kept all the regulations. I still have the option to pursue a voluntary certification, though not required by law. But there is another little catch, in that, unless I am certified, I cannot use that spiffy green and white, organic seal/logo on my labels. Is this important to my sales from the production of eighteen hives? Perhaps not.

But what if I expand? What if my little hobby becomes a, "hobby on steroids," even growing to the level that provides a nice, sideline income or even becomes so incredibly lucrative that I quit my regular, day job and throw myself into the world of commercial beekeeping?

OMG! Somebody pinch me, I think I'm dreaming!

In general, before we get into specifics, the USDA regulations require a producer to 1) prevent the commingling of organic products with non-organic products or contact with prohibited substances, 2) refrain from using the USDA organic seal and meet other organic labeling requirements without first obtaining organic certification, 3) maintain records for at least three years to prove the organic quality of the products as organically produced and handled.

But there is a transition period. Any land used to produce raw organic commodities must not have had prohibited substances applied to it for the past three years. We'll touch on this in then next section pertaining to where you set up your apiary. Until the full 36-month transition period is met, a producer may not sell, label, or represent any product as, "organic," nor use the USDA organic seal.

There is also a transition period for the honey bees. According to Section 205.240(a)(1), Bee products from an apiculture operation that are to be sold, labeled, or represented as organic must be from colonies and hives which have been under continuous organic management for no less than one year prior to the removal of the bee products from the hive.

At the beginning of the one year transition, foundation wax (if used) must be replaced and all brood comb must be new and produced by bees under organic management.

To pursue the certification process, a producer will first, supply a written, detailed description of the operation to be certified, second, a history of substances applied to the land during the past three years, third, a list of all the crops grown, raised or processed organically, and fourth, the Organic System Plan describing the practices, management and substances to be used to produce the crop. This is Section 205.201.

People often ask us if our honey is organic. Because we gross over $5,000 per year, I am automatically placed in the level that requires a written OSP and certification. But as much as I would like to manage my bees and handle my honey organically, my bees fly into areas that are not managed organically and sprayed with synthetic substances prohibited under the organic standards.

So our answer is, "No, our honey is not organic." Because of the regulations to guarantee a level playing field and to insure consumer confidence, I can't wink and say, "But we treat our bees organically, so I guess that it is!"

To adhere to the rules means we cannot insinuate or suggest our honey is organic, and technically, we cannot even tell a potential consumer our honey is, "as organic as possible." And I'm not going to delve into the, "non-certified organic," facade just because I'm unable to follow the rules. My environment where I locate my apiaries stinks with chemicals. I really have no options in this regard.

But there are two sides to this organic issue and one of them is the way we produce our honey, with the second side concerning how we market our honey. When it comes to marketing, we cannot use the, "organic," label because the land around us and the farmers who produce crops on that land use prohibited chemicals. Sadly, unless I buy or find a way to rent or control a section of land that is 3 miles wide and 3 miles long, I'm just plain out of luck.

However, if I desire to be a conscientious beekeeper, and my concern for my bees and the integrity of honey as a pure product moves me to care for my bees organically, then I have a different motivation. And this is where I want to take the rest of this manuscript.

By USDA standards, organic beekeeping is next to impossible to have certified. But what if my motivation is not stuck on appeasing my government officials, and instead satisfies my own conscience that I'm treating my bees in a humane fashion? The government has set an impossibly high bar to jump over, in order that I may have permission to use the word, "organic."

But what if it was just up to me? And what if I was just interested in satisfying my own desires to be organic, even if it was, "*as organic as possible*."

It's the difference between living by the letter of the law and the spirit of the law. And I hear a lot of distrust about government regulations and the oversight of Big Brother.

And just to yank your chain a little more, a lot of organic crop producers are all up in arms regarding, "Roundup® Ready," crops that tolerate the application of the glyphosate herbicide.

Did you know, by the government's standards, according to the Environmental Protection Agency, (EPA), that glyphosate is classified as an organic solid? And yet, the USDA prohibits the use of Roundup® for certified organic crop production. This exclusion may have resulted from the other surfactants in Roundup® which are also non-selectively toxic to weeds.

Further, the toxicity of glyphosate is incredibly low when applied to honey bees. It is promoted as biodegradable. Roundup® does not harm the honey bees.

However, it's the farmers who apply Roundup® to their crops that put honey bees in peril. How is this so?

Honey bees benefit from a floral diversity. Ask any middle-aged person like myself, one who used to walk fields of soybeans and early corn as a teenager, and we can tell you the host of flowering weeds that used to bloom in our agricultural crops, not to mention all the fence rows and corners of the fields.

But with the advent of glyphosate-based herbicides, all the weeds are wiped out, including the milkweed, a favorite mid-summer bloom for the honey bees and an integral plant in the development of the monarch butterfly. Because the fence rows are being cleaned and sanitized of their weeds, the monarch butterfly is in decline.

We forget how all this stuff is inter-related, and impacts the connectedness of life. And this is but another reason why I lean toward organic principles. I have no problem with our modern production of food. We're trying to feed a hungry planet with an expanding population. But our system of production is often called, "agrichemical," and, "chemiculture."

I can't change this reality. It is what it is. Still, I have that growing uneasiness how everything in life is inter-related on multiple levels.

Chapter 4:

Locating Your Apiaries

Section 205.240(d) states, "The producer must maintain colonies on land that is managed in accordance with the provisions in Section 205.202 through Section 205.207. All apiaries and transportation activities must be included in the OSP and approved prior to movement."

I think the most important factor to beekeeping success, whether organic or not, is the same secret to real estate success: Location, Location, Location.

I also find most beginning beekeepers acquire equipment and bees before they give serious consideration to where they're going to establish those hives. Many beginners assume their back yard is the best place, like right next to the swing set where their children play or back by the fence next to the property line where their neighbor likes to mow and string-trim the weeds. Then reality hits and the hives have to be moved, which in my experience, is no fun. The bees don't like it either.

At the farmer's markets, I've encountered many customers who entreat me to put bees on their farm or acreage. They usually try and sweeten the pot by telling me they have a fifty-square foot garden and two apple trees (as if that was all-sufficient for honey bees). And they give no thought to those pesticides they use in that garden to kill the tomato worms that might also be poisonous to the bees (you can bet they are!). They also have no clue as to what the surrounding farmers are using on their fields.

I've learned to ask some important questions, when it comes to locating an apiary. I've detailed my experience on, "back yards and out yards," in another resource which I've entitled, *"Beekeeping 101: Where Can I Keep My Bees?"* which can be purchased at

https://www.createspace.com/4044187

In your quest to be organic, or raise bees organically, you'll need to start writing an OSP, or "organic systems plan." In this plan, you'll put all the pieces of your operation together, in order to be accountable to the NOP requirements. One of those first pieces is the location of your apiary. Where will you keep your bees?

When it comes to organic beekeeping, your choice of location is significant. First, if you want to aim for certification (which you'll immediately find out is impossible), the location must meet very strict requirements, but second, you need a location that does not expose your bees to environmental toxins or drifting pesticide applications, while still meeting a season-long diversity of floral sources.

I am blessed to have several locations where my bees sit on CRP ground, which is the, "set-aside," acreage under the Conservation Reserve Program where farmers are paid not to plant. There are rules about when these plots can be mowed, but in the course of the growing season, they become verdant meadows of wild flowers and weeds. There are no livestock issues and no pesticide sprays.

Many of these areas sit among wooded lots, close to cattle pastures and hay fields, with ample weeds blooming in the fence rows and around the cattle ponds. Many of these farms sit adjacent to Interstate 55 where the shoulders and median strips are allowed to grow and bloom. I am, on occasion, questioned by potential customers at the farmer's markets, "Well, but don't you worry about all that pollution from the freeway?"

Sure I do. But is that pollution limited to those locations along the freeway? Does it not float around with the wind? Is this pollution worse than the pesticides sprayed in the fields?

I have no idea. But I do know this: my bees do very well along Interstate 55. The hives are quite productive. If pollution is a problem, and if the honey bee is the proverbial, "canary in the coal mine," than this coal mine seems to be safe.

But, as beneficial and productive as I find these locations to be for my bees and my honey production, they do not qualify as organic. So what kind of location qualifies for organic honey production?

First, anyone aspiring to organic apiculture must develop a map of the area surrounding their apiary. Most agricultural offices (county extension service, USDA, ASCS office, Farm Service) have printed, paper, county maps. Your local library should have a plat map in the Reserve Section which you can copy. An excellent on-line resource for aerial maps can be found under Google Maps on the Internet.

The purpose of the map to find your prospective location and place it at the center of the map. You need to identify what's around you. If you have multiple apiaries, you need to map out each location.

There are two major zones that are found by drawing two concentric circles from the apiary. The first circle has a radius of 1.8 miles, or 3 km. This is called your Forage Zone and covers the most likely area your bees are going to fly.

A second circle is drawn from the apiary with a radius of 2.2 miles, or 3.4 km. This outer ring is called the Surveillance Zone and will be remotely foraged by the bees, unless, of course, the plant varieties are not available in the closer Forage Zone.

One of the requirements of OSP is to show how this forage zone produces sufficient nectar sources all season long. You must list the plant species and when they bloom, and the number of acres available to the bees.

The Surveillance Zone does not have to be organically managed, but you must show what's growing in this outer ring does not pose a threat to your organic production.

We can assume, if sufficient forage is available in the Forage Zone, then the Surveillance Zone will be of minimal importance and impact. Still, you need to know what's there and note everything in your OSP.

This is no small task.

So how much land does this cover? The Forage Zone covers 6,511 acres, and the Surveillance Zone adds another 3,215 more acres, covering a total of 9,726 acres. That's a lot of ground, a lot of potential forage, and a lot of possible exclusions which will keep you from organic production.

Here's where I chuckle to myself. First, my operation entails around thirty different locations, so I'd have to draw thirty different maps, though with each location requiring a circle of 2.2 miles, I'm going to have some overlap with my other, adjacent apiaries. If I have a neighbor who also keeps bees, and does not keep them organically, this location will not qualify as one of my organic apiaries.

I need to drive around and note each field, each crop, the window of bloom, the forage density that will support a specific number of colonies, with notes on my colony numbers and their respective strengths, the soil types and topography, and which fields are under cultivation and which are left untilled.

And this has to be done on every acre in those circles.

Second, after I map out all the crops grown, I need to interview each landlord, tenant and farmer to inquire what materials they applied to these fields. This is where I break out with hysterical laughter. In my part of the world in southeast Missouri, showing up at the door of any farmer with a clipboard and a map is guaranteed to draw deep suspicion, even if I explain my motives for organic production.

To qualify as an approved location, the crops must be cultivated by organic standards. This requirement for the land and crop cultivation has requirements for soil fertility, erosion control, weed control and the choice of untreated seeds and organically produced root stock. These requirements are listed in Sections 205.202 through 205.207.

Further, I have to create a list of all the production inputs for the last three years. Some synthetic substances may be used, primarily if they do not come into contact with the crops grown, and do not contribute to the contamination of the crop, soil or water.

These allowed substances may include alcohols, chlorine materials, copper sulfate when used as an algicide, hydrogen peroxide, soap-based algicides, newspaper mulches (without colored, glossy inks), boric acid, sulfer, insecticidal soaps and herbicides, to name a few.

When it comes to non-synthetic substances, the prohibited list includes ash, arsenic, calcium chloride, lead salts, sodium nitrate, strychnine and tobacco dust (nicotine sulfate).

But the real kicker for me and my beekeeping operation is the prohibition of treated seeds, seeds from genetically modified or engineered crops, and synthetic fertilizers.

Let's see what the NOP has to say from the apicultural practice standard, Section 205.240(d) and (e):

(d) The producer must maintain colonies on land that is managed in accordance with the provisions in Section 205.202 through Section 205.207. All apiaries and transportation activities must be included in the OSP and approved prior to movement.

(e) The producer must provide bees with water and organic feed by:

(1) managing the forage zone as certified organic (either as crops or wild harvest) under the provisions of 205.202 through 205.207

(2) recognizing that bees from the operation may occasionally and minimally forage on non-organic land in the surveillance zone. The Organic System Plan must demonstrate that sufficient organic forage is available within the forage zone throughout the year. Given that even in well-managed operations with sufficient forage in the forage zone, a small number of bees will travel out of the forage zone to forage, the OSP must also demonstrate the crops in surveillance zone offer minimal risk to organic integrity.

The truth is, as I look at my maps, even if I had only one farmer plant or treat the fields within my zones with a prohibited substance, the whole 9,726 acres will fail to qualify as organic.

But the harsh reality is, in my area, my neighbors and friends are not concerned about organic crop and livestock production. They farm and raise their crops conventionally with synthetic fertilizer and treated seed, and I'll bet they don't even know if that seed is genetically modified or not.

Thus, the surrounding areas encircling my apiaries cannot be certified as organic. Not that I blame or criticize my neighbors. They have a right to farm as they see fit, just like I have a right to keep bees as I see fit.

And unless you live at the North Pole, or personally own 10,000 acres of organically managed crops, most of us are just plain out of luck. There is no way to fit into the strict compliance regulations.

So, with that bad news, the ability to get certified is out the door. But let's not give up our hopes and dreams to be, _as organic as possible_. There are other components to this vision that are more within our control.

There are two sides to this organic coin, one being the environment surrounding my apiary; the second is the environment within the hive that results from my management decisions. This is the part that is within our control

Chapter 5:

The Hive Bodies

For the majority of us beekeepers, the location of our apiary and the surrounding forage zone will exclude us from a certified organic operation based on the unavoidably normal, chemical usage within that zone. I suppose there are some remote locations that may qualify, but sadly, most of us don't live in those locations. Chemicals are everywhere and their applications seem to be a daily habit engaged by most agricultural producers and likely every suburban homeowner.

Our chemical situation is so bad, that someone once said, "If the honey was produced in America, you can bet it isn't organic."

This environmental component of organic production is out of our control and represents the biggest obstacle to certification. Still, if it is your passion to be organic and manage your bees organically, if not for certification but rather for your own conscience and peace of mind, I highly encourage you to pursue that passion by the means that are within your control.

So, presuming the environment surrounding our apiary excludes us from certification and the legitimate claim of producing organic honey, let's shift to the factors within our control, namely, the ways we raise bees and produce a crop of honey. You still cannot call your operation, "organic," but perhaps you will sleep better at night knowing you're putting the welfare of the bees ahead of any commercial gain.

If the environment within the forage zone is impossible and full of chemicals and prohibited substances, let's narrow our focus. Let's take a look at our management on the property where we keep our bees. Whether this is our back yard or our farm, do we utilize organic practices in our gardens, on our lawns, or in and around our livestock and pets?

I always think of one of my landlords who wanted bees on their farm so I could provide them with, "pesticide-free honey." Yet fifty yards from my hives was their garden where the wife dusted her zucchini with Sevin®. So I guess it's okay to use chemicals in the garden and still produce this mythical, pesticide-free honey.

If you want to be organic as possible, first consider what you do on your own property, or if a landlord allows your hives on their property, have you informed them of your organic ideals and how they need to reduce and eliminate their use of chemicals?

Let's move on with the hive and what the NOP requires. Whether we keep bees in a conventional

Langstroth hive, a top bar hive (TBH), a Warre hive or any variation of the possibilities, a hive must be made from non-synthetic materials. This requirement will automatically exclude polystyrene hives, most commonly marketed under the BeeMax® brand name, and sold by the majority of beekeeping suppliers.

Just for the record, I own six BeeMax® hives which I bought for my own research and evaluation. These hives must be painted with a latex paint to resist ultra-violet degradation from the sun. They don't rot, but large, black ants have no reluctance boring sizable holes into the cracks between hive bodies.

Personally, I kind of like these BeeMax® hives, but they are not cheap. When I'm looking to acquire more hive bodies, I'm more likely to make my own hives out of scrap wood and the economic advantage it provides than purchase new.

There are other manufacturers of polystyrene hives, a Danish company called, Swienty, to name one, which are sometimes mistakenly called, "STYROFOAM™" hives (www.swienty.com).

You can also run an Internet search for styrofoam beehives and you'll find Beevilla, (www.beevilla.com), Beaver Plastics, (www.bpgrower.com), or Beebox by Paradise Honey, (www.paradisehoney.fi).

By the way, the STYROFOAM™ Brand name is a registered trademark of The Dow Chemical Company, frequently misused as a generic term for disposable foam products such as coffee cups, coolers and packaging materials. These materials, however, are made from expanded polystyrene products. Still, beekeepers will refer to polystyrene hives generically as, "styrofoam," and they won't qualify for organic production, which seems to be a no-brainer for me.

As an aside, since I keep bees in BeeMax® hives, if I chose to have a certified organic honey production, I would have to take great pains to keep my organic production completely segregated from any non-organic production. The NOP guidelines refer to this kind of dual-system as a, "split operation."

As I said in the last chapter, the OSP must clearly address the management practices that prevent commingling and contamination between the two operations, from production all the way to harvest and extraction and storage. The OSP must also address any potential commingling resulting from bee drift and robbing. I think this is best accomplished by keeping non-organic apiaries out of the forage and surveillance zones, and at a minimum 2.2 miles from the organic apiary.

The Walter T. Kelley Beekeeping Company has for many years marketed hive components made of hard plastic. This plastic material also does not qualify if you want to define your management as organic. I have many of these components that I've acquired over the years from retiring beekeepers, and while they are impervious to rot and decay, they are prone to warp. Mother Lode

Products, (www.motherlodeproducts.com), also manufactures plastic equipment.

Metal, specifically used for queen excluders, screen bottom boards and outer covers is allowed under the organic protocols.

Hives must be made of non-synthetic materials, the most common material being wood. There is no specific species of wood suggested or required under the organic protocols, but the most common wood sold for bee hives is pine, though cedar and cypress are frequently sold in catalogs. The latter two woods are more resistant to decay and rot than the former, and pine is certainly easier to work.

There are no requirements where this wood is obtained, i.e., a big-box retailer like Lowes or Home Depot. There are no requirements that the wood come from a tree felled in an organically managed forest. With increasing threats from the Emerald Ash Borer in our part of the country, I'm surprised some of these trees do not carry insecticidal residues all the way through the milling process. Commercial wood is shiny and smooth, that after planing and sanding, a, "mill glaze," covers the board.

As I said earlier, I'm more prone to build my own boxes out of scrap lumber which I may acquire from farm implement dealers, restaurant supply houses or signage companies. There was a day and age in my early years when I had more time than money. I would drive the back alleys and loading docks searching for packing crates, which oddly, was often a better grade of wood than I could buy from the big-box retailers...and the price was right!

If you want my whole story of my beekeeping vision, check out this resource, *"Beekeeping With Twenty-five Hives,"* https://www.createspace.com/4152725

In my book, *"Beekeeping With Twenty-five Hives,"* I also go into the advantages and benefits of searching for used equipment, and since I had no knowledge of the previous beekeeper's management practices for miticides, and no knowledge of where he kept his bees (with potential to pesticide exposure), I do not know how anyone can acquire used equipment and make plans for a legitimate organic apiary.

There is no requirement to paint the hives, but if left bare and unprotected, one must simply anticipate the wood will need replacement after a given period of time. There is a belief that organic requirements insist on unpainted wood, but this is not true, according to the NOP standards.

There is no distinction in the organic requirements between latex or enamel paints. Most beekeepers know to paint the outside of the hive bodies, leaving the inside surfaces unpainted. Still, some of the used equipment I've picked up over the years is painted, inside and out.

A nice, water-based product is Eco-Wood, (http://www.ecowoodtreatment.com) sold by the Walter T. Kelley Company, (www.kelleybees.com).

Obviously, any commercially-treated wood is prohibited, and Section 205.206(f) specifically declares that, "a producer must not use lumber treated with arsenate or other prohibited materials for new installations or replacement purposes in contact with soil or livestock."

Sections 205.601 through 205.604 provide the complete list of prohibited and allowed substances, but as it pertains to treated lumber, Chromated Copper Arsenate (CCA), Alkaline Copper Quaternary (ACQ), Acid Copper Chromate (ACC), and Copper azole (CBA) were the most popular treated wood options available commercially, all of which, are prohibited.

Wood treated with CCA was discontinued in 2003 for residential use due to the unsafe health concerns. Even when wood treated with CCA is burned, some of the arsenic is volatized in the fire, but the ash remains a hazardous waste.

By 2005, many of the commercially available preservatives had been regulated out, and new formulations have taken their place. If you desire certification, the best advice to give is to work closely with your certifying agent and the development of your Organic System Plan (OSP). Newer synthetic formulations are typically not on either list, prohibited or allowed, because they have not been evaluated by the National Organic Standards Board (NOSB), nor have they been petitioned for inclusion on the National List. This leaves a grey area that must be satisfied in consultation with the certifying agent if this is the direction you are heading.

Though not normally available, I still find pressure-treated wood products in use on various farms, even as hive stands which elevate the hive from the potential decay of damp soil. I've seen quite a number of bottom boards made from pressure-treated plywood, which makes sense to reduce the rot, but not for organic purposes. Many of these hive stands and bottom boards are purchased from retiring beekeepers and continue in use, due, in part, to the wonderful resilience and longevity of CCA treated lumber.

Once in a blue moon, you'll find stacks of unused, pressure-treated lumber at farm auctions, previously stored away under the protection of sheds and barns for a future use that never materialized. This chemical treatment was the industry standard since the 1930s and much of it is, shockingly, still in use for lovely applications like children's playground equipment and landscaping boards many homeowners use in their gardens.

If you choose to paint your hives, only the outside surface may be painted with a non-lead based paint. Lead is added to paint to speed up drying, increase durability, maintain a fresh appearance, and resist moisture that causes corrosion. While enamel paints may contain a number of synthetic, toxic solvents, namely mineral spirits and toluene, the regulatory bans since 1978 in the United States make lead based paint impossible to purchase.

Again, there is no distinction in the organic requirements between latex or enamel paints, but if I was seriously aiming for an organic production, my money is on latex paint. It's also easier to clean up and when I paint, I make a mess. There are no regulations which restrict your color choices.

Again, in my resource, *Beekeeping with Twenty-five Hives,* I share my experience with mistint paint in the bargain bin at just about any paint store or big-box retailer. Part of my methodology is to paint a hive with the most garish, grotesque color of paint that no self-respecting thief would bother stealing it. Unfortunately, garish colors like pinks and orange make apiaries more noticeable. Thus far...knock on wood...my apiaries have not been bothered by thieves or vandals.

However, if you hang out at farm auctions, estate sales or frequent the used construction businesses like Habitat for Humanity's, "ReStore," outlets, it is not out of the realm of possibilities to find cans and buckets of old paint and stain, some partially used and some which have not even been opened, some of which date back before 1978. I prefer to stick with new, latex paint.

As an alternative to paint, a non-synthetic wood preservative may be used on the exterior surfaces. The most commonly available wood preservative is linseed oil. Linseed oil comes in raw or boiled versions. Raw linseed oil has a slower drying time than boiled linseed oil but does not contain synthetic solvents to speed the rate of drying. Either raw or boiled linseed oil will require another treatment in three to four years, and once dried, wood treated with linseed oil may be painted.

Linseed oil is a nice alternative to paint and leaves a beautiful, weathered appearance without warping or surface degradation.

As an experiment, I tried several of the popular, relatively inexpensive, homeowner grade, deck and fence preservatives. They are disappointing with poor durability, hardly lasting one full season before the wood oxidizes, looking dry, cracked and weathered.

Even if you're not gearing up for organic practices, these big-box preservatives are not suited for bee hives (think, Thompson's WaterSeal) which seal moisture into the wood, and as long as you have moisture, you create a perfect environment for rot and insects.

If you are looking for a commercially-prepared, non-toxic preservative, check out your local lumber yard or hardware store for Cedarshield made by *www.CedarSiders.com*, or call (877) 669-0482. Cedarshield is a one-time, lifetime, non-aqueous penetrant, wood stabilizer. Wood can be painted once dry. It is also available on *www.amazon.com*.

If you are searching for a commercially prepared, exterior wood preservative, you have three natural choices that I know of, none of which, at this time, have been added or prohibited to the National List.

Again, these treatments would have to be evaluated and petitioned for inclusion, or thoroughly discussed with your certifying agent...if that's the route you want to go. Obviously, if you are not shooting for a certification, you'll have to evaluate these preservatives on their own merit and your level of comfort. Read the ingredient list carefully, especially the warnings for skin contact and fumes.

The first is a product manufactured by Bioshield Paint Company of Santa Fe, New Mexico, called "Wood Impregnation #99." From the information provided on their website, Bioshield manufactures paints, stains, thinners, and waxes that are made form such naturally derived materials citrus peel oils and solvents, essential oils, seed oils, tree resins, inert mineral fillers, tree and bee waxes, lead-free dryers, and earth pigments. Check their website at *www.bioshieldpaint.com*, or call, (800) 621-2591.

A second product is "AURO #121 Natural Resin Oil Primer," which penetrates the wood deeply to protect from within, is applied as a thin coat and followed up by a stain or varnish. It is distributed by Sinan Company of Davis, California, which also distributes other natural products manufactured from natural raw materials including an organically grown linseed oil (not diluted with any kind of petroleum products). Their web address is *www.dcn.davis.ca.us/go/sinan*, or call, (530) 753-3104.

A third option is, "Lifetime Wood Treatment," manufactured by Valhalla Wood Preservatives, Ltd., in Calgary, Alberta, Canada. This product has no known toxic effects as it is made from naturally occurring plant and mineral substances. It is supposed to be a one-time application and will not leach into soil or water. Information can be obtained from *www.valhalco.com* or call, (403) 228-5193.

A fourth option is to make your own preservative. A very common, public domain recipe (meaning no one has copyright or trademark rights to it) was developed by the USDA's Forest Products Laboratory. The original recipe calls for paraffin wax, a petroleum derivative which is prohibited in Section 205.105 (c) of the NOP. You could substitute carnauba or wood rosin wax, perhaps even bees wax. I prefer paraffin for the cost and availability, even though it is not organically approved.

Carefully melt 1 ounce of paraffin (or the other alternative options) in a double boiler. It's not much, but it is flammable. Once melted, move away from the heat source, preferably outdoors or in a well-ventilated area, and vigorously stir 14-1/2 cups of a solvent, adding the melted paraffin slowly while stirring. This solvent may be distilled pine tar, mineral spirits, paint thinner, turpentine or citrus thinner. I prefer turpentine.

Once dissolved, add 1-1/2 cups of boiled linseed oil to make a full gallon. Obviously, wear whatever protective equipment you deem necessary, and don't be sloppy and make a mess, avoid breathing the fumes, and avoid contact with your skin and eyes.

This formulation can be brushed on or the wood can be dipped. I bought a large, plastic storage tote from Wal-Mart, big enough to hold my brood boxes and bottom boards. I pour two gallons of my mixture in the tote, then set the hive body on its side into the mixture.

As I rotate the different sides out of the mix, I use a stiff brush to work the solution into the exposed ends, giving every side about thirty seconds per soak, allowing each side two soakings. Each box takes about five minutes and once thoroughly dried, can be painted. They take about a week in good sunshine to thoroughly dry.

This formula may be fortified with Copper-8-quinolinolate, available from *www.chemservice.com*, $96.70 for a 500 mg container (yeah, that's kind of pricey). However, this treatment, also called, "oxine copper," is the only EPA-registered wood preservative permitted by the U.S. Food and Drug Administration for treatment of wood used in direct contact with food. It has low toxicity to humans and animals, but is very resilient to fungi and rot.

A second option to fortify your preservative is Copper Napthenate, which, like Copper-8-quinolinolate, is an organometalic compound. Copper Napthenate is fairly safe to use, represents low toxicity to humans and animals, and is available locally in small, economical units at most hardware or big-box home improvement centers, and from some of the beekeeping supply catalogs. It has a long history of safe applications and was at one time the most widely used wood preservative in the beekeeping industry.

However, when you talk to some of these old timers, especially the old commercial beekeepers, they loved to mix Copper Napthenate with #2 diesel fuel and soak the hive components for twenty-four hours.

Seriously. Diesel fuel! And remember how I warned you about buying used equipment?

You have many options for your hive components. At one time, my only plan to provide longevity was latex paint. Sadly, even with two coats of paint, and in some cases, preceded with a good primer, my brood boxes and supers still rotted at the corners and finger joints.

Then I got lazy and left a batch of my newly purchased boxes unpainted with similarly poor results. Though I initially enjoyed the naturally weathered finish, they started cracking and splitting.

With the need to save money on replacement boxes, I started using the boiled linseed oil, paraffin and turpentine formulation, and once dry, I opted to paint the boxes with a high quality, oil-based enamel that I find at my local ReStore outlet. An excellent paint is floor and porch paint, though I have little choice in the color selection. My preference is subtle earth tones, browns and greens to avoid unwanted attention from strangers.

So you have different options, including doing nothing for your woodware. Whatever your choice, the most logical place to start is with the health of the bees and the fumes from any treatment that may pose a risk.

The second factor would be longevity, not just of the wood but also from the treatment, and raw linseed oil requires further applications down the road.

Now that we have our hives situated, the next step is frames and foundation.

Chapter 6:

Frames and Foundations

Our current beekeeping industry is in a pickle. Every supply company catering to beekeepers sells wax foundation, wired or otherwise, which are the sheets of embossed bees wax that fit in our frames. The purpose of foundation is to give the bees a template from which they'll draw out the comb for brood production and nectar ripening.

In reality, the bees use the wax in these sheets as the initial resource to begin drawing out the comb. Though we give them a template, mostly worker sized cells, I've had colonies simply rework the size of the cells to fit their needs, mostly resizing the cells for drone production.

So who supplies the wax to these companies who make the foundation? We believe a large portion of this wax comes from the large-scale, commercial beekeepers, many of whom utilize chemical treatments in their management of colonies.

Additionally, many of these commercial beekeepers pollinate orchards and crops contaminated with synthetic fertilizers, pesticides, insecticides and herbicides. The exposure to the bees brings untold contaminants into the hive where they take up residence in the wax comb.

At this point, it is not my objective to condone or berate the commercial aspects of our industry that have grown with and accommodated a chemically-dependent agricultural production system. This is one of the many factors of our food chain I cannot control and making a fuss won't change a thing.

Many of my contemporaries and peers, in both beekeeping and crop production and marketing, also lament the chemical dependency of modern agriculture. Chemical pesticides are perceived as the main culprit of hive mortality, but no one seems to believe there is an alternative, irrespective of what organic crop production can offer in terms of equivalent yields.

While the consensus of beekeepers focuses generically on pesticides, my attention concentrates on the chemical residues that seep into the wax comb in the hive. As large-scale beekeepers render their wax, the chemical pesticides remain and are processed into sheets of foundation, and then sold to small beekeepers like you and me.

Unknown for many years, many of us small scale beekeepers have been introducing chemical residues into our hives every time we purchased commercially-prepared foundation. What effects those residues have is still under scrutiny, but we know they affect queen fertility and drone sperm viability. I'll bet that was an interesting project to try and run past a dissertation committee.

Further, as we test the sheets of foundation, we are finding residues of legally-registered miticides, and some kitchen sink concoctions that have no business in a bee hive.

Part of the problem is what commercial beekeepers use to combat the varroa mites, and many of these chemicals are legally-registered and considered safe for the honey bee. But these miticides are leaving residues that accumulate every year the comb remains in the colony, and every year the hive is treated for mites.

Part of the problem is the physiology of the honey bee as she forages the blooms. As the worker flies through our polluted environment, her hairy body naturally attracts statically-charged particles of pollutants in the air. She's like a flying broom sampling the environment and harvesting the contaminants along with the pollen. As she drinks from the creeks and cattle ponds, she ingests the chemical run-off from countless acres of modern, production agriculture.

Some beekeepers have had the idea of producing organic bees wax, free of chemicals. Rather than starting out with chemically-tainted commercial foundation, they placed bees in pristine new hives with new frames lacking the conventional, commercially prepared, bees wax foundation.

The beekeeping community refers to this method as, "foundationless frames," or in some cases denoted as, "FF." It is as if the bees were a swarm that took up residence in a hollow tree and started their construction with clean wax, made from scratch from their wax glands.

To the chagrin of the beekeepers, once the wax in these pristine, clean hives was sampled and tested, many pathogens and chemical impurities turned up in the analysis. Dumbfounded, they looked at each other and pondered where these contaminants came from.

Some of them were known miticides that could have only come from another bee hive. Was this the result of robbing, when one colony amorally plunders a weaker, perhaps wild colony within the forage zone? Are some of these chemicals used for other problems in other crops? Has wind or rain brought a chemical drift into our forage zone? Did a bee from a treated hive leave a chemical residue on a flower that another bee picked up later?

And I can honestly say, "I don't know."

What I do know is chemicals are everywhere, so much, that the manufacturer of a line of health products marked as Burt's Bees®, is rumored to only buy their bees wax from foreign sources and not from beekeepers in the United States. Our bees wax is polluted. Chemicals are everywhere.

Now that's a powerful statement to the degree of pollution we tolerate, every day, and the potential threat to our bees. Then I start imagining what threats we bring to our consumers in that bottle of honey.

The NOP protocols state that any wax used for organic beekeeping may be sourced from organic foundation (okay, where are you going to get that, except from foreign sources like Burt's Bees®), plastic foundation dipped in organic or conventional wax, or organic or conventional wax. Once the entire apiary has been converted to organic production, all plastic foundation must be dipped in organic wax.

The inclusion of plastic foundation, even if covered with organic wax, challenges my comprehension. Make no mistake, I love plastic foundation for the durability and ease of use, but I personally don't consider it organic. I do, however, cover all my plastic foundation with my own bees wax, but I use a 4" foam paint roller to apply my wax rather than dipping. The NOP protocols are pretty clear when they ask plastic frames be dipped.

I am of the opinion that it takes a strong nectar flow and a pretty stout colony to successfully draw out plastic foundation, and most colonies are reluctant to do so. I sought to encourage comb building so I apply melted bees wax with a foam roller. The wax application provides a nice base which the bees will use to start drawing the comb. The problem, however, is that I cannot produce organic bees wax. Again, my ideals of embracing the NOP standards for organic apiculture miss the target.

As a side note, the NOP protocols do not include any mention of all-in-one, plastic frame and foundation, sometimes referred to as, "Pierco," frames.

Pierco is the brand name of one of several manufacturers of molded, plastic frames that include the foundation as a one-piece unit. I still find the addition of my bees wax eases the process of drawing out the plastic foundation, and if I get lazy and avoid it, there will be issues as some plastic foundation is totally ignored.

I think the application to take to heart is the incredible level of pollutants within the forage zone that cannot be minimized or ignored. When the organic protocols demand an accounting of every acre of production and every input applied on these crops, the requirement seems insurmountable. And yet, as much as we want to declare our apiaries to be organic, even _as organic as possible_, we have to concede the environment representing the forage zone renders an ominous threat, a real and present danger, to our organic desires, not to mention our bees, maybe even to our existence as beekeepers.

At this juncture, I'm tempted to offer a mild expletive and dramatically vociferate with an appropriate inflection, **"It is impossible to produce organic honey and manage my bees organically."**

And I think I'm correct.

However, as impossible as it is to declare our production as organic, let's simmer down and look at what we can control, namely our frames and foundation. Just within this small aspect of managing our colonies, how can we best fulfill the organic requirements, given the crappy environment which is silently poisoning everything that lives and breathes and struggles for existence?

Okay, maybe that's a little too much dramatic vociferating.

The organic protocols for frames and foundations begins with wood frames. Let's start with brand new frames that we presume free of contaminants. The easiest method of avoiding deliberate contamination from chemical residues is to steer clear of purchasing commercial sheets of foundation. Let's go with foundationless frames, which are also an excellent way to let the bees draw out the size of cells they desire.

Foundationless frames, while not part of the NOP protocols, offers a nice compromise. Yes, our environment is polluted, and the wax comb drawn from foundationless frames will be polluted.

However, the burning question in my mind ponders which is the lesser of two evils, the commercially-prepared wax foundation with the commercial residues, or the wax comb built out on the foundationless frames? I have a hunch, which is totally ignorant, that the foundationless frames will be a better choice. As you look around your apiaries, you will also gather that gut-level hunch if your environment is clean enough, free of commercial agriculture, such that it favors foundationless frames. What comes to my mind is the CRP acres in the set aside program, also called Conservation Reserve Program. They are generally left fallow and host a variety of floral diversity. There is no need for pesticides. These apiary locations suit me, just fine.

Foundationless frames also have the benefit of allowing the colony to draw out their preferred cell size. Healthy colonies tend to draw out too much drone comb, in our humble opinion, and thus we tend to favor those sheets embossed with worker-sized cells. Beekeepers, especially beginners, tend to over-react with histrionics about the amount of drone comb drawn out by a colony and how really strong colonies will rework the worker-sized cells into drone comb.

To a beginner, drone comb represents an unproductive bee, a literal parasite in this matriarchal society. Drone comb also is preferred by the maternal varroa mite that slides in on the day the cell is sealed for pupation so she can lay eggs. Since drones take twenty-four days to gestate when compared to the twenty-one days for a worker, the population of varroa mites accelerates with more drone comb.

When pressed about the problem of excess drone comb, I usually take a deep breath and tell myself to relax prior to answering the concerns. Drone comb is the sign of a healthy colony with sufficient worker population (a priority) that must be established before drone comb is drawn.

When left to their own choices, a colony senses the need for drones based on the time of year and the seasonality of the queen breeding season. Somewhere we need to stop our incessant micro-management of the bees and give them a little credit for something they've been doing for a million years. They have ways of handling the need for drones.

Foundationless frames, giving the bees a choice in the cell size, what we might want to call, "natural" cell size, then push the discussion to frames with what we call, "small cells."

If normal worker cells on sheets of embossed wax foundation run in the 5.2 to 5.4 mm range, small cell management seeks to regress the bee back to what nature intended in the 4.9 mm size. Or so we think this is the size bees used to be before we messed up nature's design.

Small cell discussions open the door to the debate how beekeepers thought a larger bee would gather more nectar and make more honey, thus, beekeepers in the opening years of the Twentieth Century deliberately pushed the cell size on the sheets of foundation to larger, "unnatural," sizes, up to 5.4 mm.

In the last decade, a push to reduce the size of the cell came to the forefront with claims smaller cells had less room for varroa mites to reproduce. The jury is still out and the many experiments have come back with mixed results and inconclusive suppositions. Cell size has no bearing on complying with the NOP standards. The use of small cell is controversial and the success of small cell foundation requires advanced management skills.

Foundationless frames, with natural cell size, will run a mixture of small and large cell sizes, worker and drones, and given the chemical residues known to exist in commercial foundation, I think foundationless frames offer a nice alternative to being *as organic as possible*, even though we have to concede our environment is awash in a lot of crap that poses threats to us all.

I've tried to shake new packages into hive bodies with ten, foundationless frames. I melted my own bees wax and affixed large, "craft sticks," purchased from Wal-Mart or any hobby store, into the space where the foundation usually is wedged. Some beekeepers will slip a strip of wax foundation under the cleat and nail it in place. I've had better luck with the craft sticks as the foundation sometimes slides out.

But with ten foundationless frames, the bees will tend to migrate from one frame over to the next. Then you have a huge headache and have to break out the comb and force the bees to start over.

I've had much greater success pulling a couple of old frames out of a brood box and alternating the new foundationless frames between two existing frames with fully drawn brood comb. The colony will draw out those frames as straight as an arrow.

Even with conventional, chemical beekeeping management, beekeepers are encouraged to change out old frames of drawn comb for new frames with new foundation as a means of reducing the amounts of chemical residues. The recommended rate is 20%, or two old frames for every brood box. The new foundation can be of wired, wax foundation, plastic foundation or foundationless.

As one of my beekeeping buddies said of this practice of rotating frames out of the brood nest, "It's like changing your socks every day. A fresh pair of socks keeps me from getting a fungus infection; and rotating comb out of my brood nest keeps my bees healthier."

The ultimate bottom line comes during the year, or years it takes to transition into the organic protocols. All the foundation wax that came with your bees, if you bought a hive or a nuc, must be replaced and rotated out with new brood comb produced by the bees under organic management.

The NOP standards seem to assume your forage zone fits the requirements for certification and does not contain contaminants from crops grown with prohibited substances, and thus, your bees will be under organic management.

Again, the significance of the forage zone comes into play. You may have an organic farm, or you may refuse to use chemicals on your garden which sits in the immediate vicinity of your apiary, but bees fly great distances, and unless you control the inputs on those crops, organic management remains elusive.

Still, if you bought a nuc or a hive from a beekeeper who utilizes chemical miticides, you'll want to rotate the original frames out and replace them. Obviously, the easier choice is to buy a package of bees and shake them out on new frames, which is where our next step in the organic journey leads us.

Chapter 7:

Acquiring Bees

When approached at the farmer's market by an inquisitive, potential beekeeper, the question always comes up, "Where can I get some bees?"

Usually, this question arises in the middle of June, when the weather is wonderful and the hives are booming. Nectar is pouring in and the last thing I'm thinking about is selling off any of my work force. I'm in the honey business. I could, and would sell some bees after the nectar flow diminishes, but of what value would those bees be for the novice beekeeper who has no knowledge of keeping a colony going during the summer dearth?

There is a seasonality to the availability of honey bees and queens, and the price reflects the supply and demand. In the early fall, usually right after Labor Day, I've seen some hives listed for sale, very reasonably priced, on places like *www.craigslist.com* on the Internet.

I believe these hives were harvested of their honey, still needing some kind of mite treatment, hence the buyer now assumes the winter risk of keeping them alive.

For the experienced beekeeper, I can see an opportunity. For the beginner, I see a potential disaster. Still, I'd much rather buy fresh nucs in the spring, even if the nuc in the spring was the same price as the full hive in the fall.

There are scads of beekeepers who are in the queen rearing business, which may also include sales of nucs and packages. While I'm not averse to selling some bees, there are beekeepers who are better equipped to advertise, handle sales, as well as deal with the follow-up questions and complaints, and replacements.

This aspect of selling bees intensifies in the early spring. Once upon a time, queen availability was limited to the spring. But since it takes several weeks to raise a queen from grafted larvae through a successful mating, queen breeders ramped up their production to meet an increasing, and often unpredictable, unprecedented demand.

Many of the leftover spring queens are simply banked and sold through the summer. I've heard second-hand stories of queen producers dumping the unsold, leftover queens as the demand going into winter dries up. I can only think, "What a waste of resources." But in reality, it's just business.

So when asked about buying bees, I like to point the inquiring beekeeper to commercial queen producers and beekeepers who sell nucs and packages.

I have in the past, in the early spring, driven to the southern regions of the country and brought up southern-raised nucs and packages to resell to my local beekeeping buddies. Because the mass-produced quantity (attempting to meet skyrocketing demand) was beyond the normal control of human observation, and because that quality was sometimes, no, many times uncertain and unchecked, not all nucs would measure up to my standards. They fell into a wide range of expectations, despite being described as, "five-frame nucs."

But when I drove down, I didn't have time to personally inspect all the nucs I was buying, either. Those nuc sellers in the south were harried and hurried taking care of people like me. They didn't seem to have the time to take care of the nucs like I hoped. I was happy to get the nucs on my trailer before I headed back to Jackson.

Because the shipping stress was severe even when I hauled them on my own carefully packed truck and trailer, the nucs and packages suffered further. And I was bringing them to a foreign land, much colder than where they were raised. I was registering my own stress with southern nucs.

Because I felt like an S.O.B. (Stupid Obstinate Beekeeper) selling a problematic nuc to a greenhorn beginner, proverbially, "still wet behind the ears," I was the one who voluntarily absorbed the dubious nucs and packages into my own apiaries. Basically, there were non-productive and negated any profits I may have incurred from selling the productive nucs.

I never wanted any dissatisfied customers, you know, the ones who end up bitching, whining and complaining that I messed them over with a crappy nuc. In our industry, reputation speaks volumes about one's personal character. I wanted a good reputation, but mostly I was in this part of the business hoping to help a beginner succeed, not forcing them to scramble to find a replacement nuc two weeks after they bought one from me.

Of course, when I sold nucs to those beginners, they wanted to visit on the driveway for two hours. They had a thousand questions and I had a million things yet to do that day.

These were many of the reasons I bailed out of reselling nucs, but local people still need bees. And secretly, I still buy a few nucs, just to have on hand to sell to those people who can't seem to get their chips together in February, or those who didn't start looking for nucs and packages until May, which is way too late to find anything available. I'm just a recovering procrastinator helping another procrastinator...or is it enabling?

And there are some of my buddies who only have a few hives. The hives survive until late-March, then die out for some reason. It's usually too late to acquire nucs and I like to be in a helpful position to help someone in need. So I will buy a few nucs or packages to refill my own winter losses, and plan on selling a few to the beekeeper who finds himself out of luck.

But for the majority of beekeepers who call me looking for nucs, I send them, with my best wishes and a little sage advice, to the commercial nuc producers.

Anything wrong with this? Well, a lot of nuc producers still use chemicals. Some of the hives coming out of places like almond pollination in California are split and sold into nucs, or shaken out into packages.

Some of the southern beekeepers are chemical beekeepers, not that I'm complaining or being disrespectful, but it's the way they raise their bees and address the hive's health issues. Volume production pushes one into an economy of scale which needs to be managed with antibiotics and treatments, unfortunately.

Thankfully, many southern nuc producers are switching over to treatment-free and chemical-free beekeeping. But these alternatives are not necessarily organic beekeeping, though it's a step in the right direction.

We've seen increasing emphasis on what we call, "Local Nuc Initiatives," where local beekeepers work to make locally adapted nucs available in the spring. This movement is slowly gaining traction. Still, locally adapted nucs do not necessarily translate into organically raised honey bees.

I like to trap feral swarms, which at one point I believe were actually unmanaged colonies living in trees and building cavities without human intervention. I believed, though it could not be proven, that these supposedly unmanaged colonies figured out how to overcome the ravages of the varroa mite.

If these bees had a genetic resistance against varroa mites, then they would be great additions to my bee yards which I attempted to manage without synthetic chemicals. It is my belief these bees are great candidates for organic management.

However, with the explosive growth in beginning beekeeping, and their lack of knowledge and management skills, we believe many swarms today originate from managed colonies, some treated with chemicals, some with bees requiring treatments.

I remember when I was a beginner, I had issues with swarming in my colonies. I'm not beating up the beginners, but with the rise in the interest of keeping bees, we have seen a parallel association with the rise in swarm sightings, especially in urban areas.

Still, I set out a number of pheromone-baited swarm traps and catch "free bees." If you're interested, you can find my resource, *"Keeping Honey Bees and Swarm*

Trapping: A Better Way to Collect Free Bees" at https://www.createspace.com/4106626

Nevertheless, the NOP protocols do not make an issue of where, or how you initially acquire your bees, whether nuc or package or hive or feral swarm. There are also no restrictions on queen honey bees.

Perhaps you already have hives you can split, hives you've been managing naturally or treatment-free, or not. Will these bees work for organic management?

The answer is yes, and no.

Actually, the organic protocols don't care where you get your bees. They will still be required to convert during a one year transition under organic production management with a rotation of comb as I outlined in chapter six.

If you wish to expand your organic apiary, you have three options. 1) You can split your organic colonies and form nucleus colonies. 2) You can find someone who manages organic colonies and purchase organic hives, bees or nucs. 3) You can purchase non-organic bees, i.e. packaged bees, and run them through the one year transition under organic management as I outlined in chapter six.

Replacement bees are just a little different. You may acquire either organic bees or non-organic bees, provided the bees from non-organic sources are limited to 25% of the colonies from the previous season. These non-organic colonies must be managed organically for a minimum of sixty days without any supers or harvest equipment.

Personally, I'm little confused. If I expand, the non-organic bees must be transitioned for one year. But if I need replacement bees, the non-organic bees need only be under organic management for sixty days without supers.

Perhaps the unwritten clarification presumes the expansion bees will come with non-organic frames that must be rotated out, and the replacement bees are packages that can be installed in a hive that I previously managed organically.

At least, that's my best guess. If I was serious about organic beekeeping, and if my forage zone could qualify for certification, this is an issue I would have to work out with my certifying agent.

There are many times, reading through the NOP standards and recommendations, that I feel the final consensus of what truly qualifies as an organic practice has not been left up to practicing beekeepers, but rather, set into law by politicians and bureaucratic administrators.

Secondly, I feel much of what constitutes organic beekeeping cannot always be predicted, calculated or foreseen. The recommendations cannot cover every whim of nature, every contingency, every possible nuance of what happens in a hive.

If you remember from your OSP, you had to describe the floral sources in the forage zone as sufficient for the number of hives. Bear in mind, you are required to list the site-specific conditions for appropriate hive densities and colony locations within that respective apiary. But every year is different and sometimes there is not enough forage.

In the event you need to feed your bees, you may provide supplemental feed from organic honey, organic sugar syrup, and/or pollen substitutes and supplements that are allowed under Section 205.603, *Except*, that, the producer must not provide organic sugar syrup less than 15 days prior to placement of the supers or any other bee product collection equipment. This is stipulated in Section 205.240(f)(1).

When it comes to bee stocks, I'm a big fan of genetically resistant, locally adapted stock, basically, "survivor" stock. Unfortunately, this word means different things to different people. It is assumed that to survive means without the aid of synthetic chemicals, maybe even treatment-free. If you are buying from a queen producer that advertises, "survivor," stock, ask what they mean and see how it fits into the NOP standards.

Hygienic behavior is another characteristic selected by queen producers. These traits are important for compliance with the NOP standards, requiring a beekeeper to select stocks resistant to prevalent diseases and pests. The use of modified equipment, such as screen bottom boards, are encouraged as a means to control pests and diseases.

I still believe the varroa mite is our biggest problem, a vector of viruses and diseases. Interestingly, the NOP standards do not encourage treatment-free management or the, "Bond method," (live and let die), which is basically benign neglect. Beekeepers may not destroy bee colonies following honey flows, either intentionally or by neglect.

The NOP standards call for the use of therapeutic applications of non-synthetic materials to control pests, parasites, and diseases, *Provided*, that such materials are not prohibited under Section 205.604; and the use of therapeutic applications of synthetic materials, *Provided*, that such materials are allowed under Section 205.603.

The NOP standards are very clear how any beekeeper must not accept the presence of pests, parasites, or disease without initiating efforts to restore the health of the colony, thus the ideals of treatment-free beekeeping do not fit the protocols of organic beekeeping.

I'm sure this rule/recommendation is going to irritate almost all of the treatment-free beekeepers who take great pride (in a humble sense) of their lack of chemical dependency which may lead them to proclaim their organic status. But remember, the overall purpose of organic beekeeping is the preservation of resources, one of which is live honey bees.

Remember, too, many of these recommendations are under review, and if certain substances are cleared by the EPA, the use of such may be petitioned and evaluated by the NOP.

One recent addition to the arsenal against varroa is formic acid. In 2010, the Hawaii State Department of Agriculture petitioned the NOSB and it was approved, solely for use on honey bees to combat varroa, added to the National List at Section 205.603(b)(2).

When it comes to smoking bees, beekeepers may not use prohibited substances in their smokers, as stated in Section 205.604. Curiously, any synthetic bee repellants may not be used to remove bees from their honey. Check the catalogs and you'll find a new trend in natural substances which have not been included in the NOP standards. I'm guessing the present NOP standards are referring to two products, BeeGo and Honey Robber.

Hives may not be rotated between organic and non-organic locations, or allow organic hives to be managed non-organically. If you move hives, you need to keep accurate records.

Beekeepers are required to maintain adequate supplies of honey and pollen in the hive, including leaving hives with reserves of honey and pollen sufficient for the colony to survive the dormancy period or during a nectar dearth. If starvation is imminent, beekeepers are required to implement their supplemental feeding plan.

Chapter 8:

Where are we at?

Ten Truths: Summary and Conclusions

So what do we know? I know that once upon a time, during the press releases announcing the establishment of a nationally uniform organic standard, I had dreams of producing and marketing organic honey. I saw a huge marketing niche missing from our store shelves.

Once I looked into the requirements, I knew such a dream was impossible, an illusory proposition. We live in a country where our industrial food production system thrives on chemical pesticides and synthetic fertilizers.

It was my late-father's lament that the soil is no longer a living entity, but has become a sterile, non-fertile carrier to hold the seed, fertilizer and insecticide as we continue to push the limits of food production to meet the demands of an increasing population.

Sadly, the consensus in the agricultural sector points to a continuation of this production system, fearing that it will not likely change until we are forced into a disruptive food revolution or apocalyptic collapse.

At one time, the advent of Colony Collapse Disorder, or CCD, also known as the, "Disappearing Bee Problem," was heralded as the prophetic, "canary in the coal mine." But that clarion call for radical social change fell on deaf ears as the dire headlines slid off of the front page of our news media.

Unfortunately, we live the adrenaline-driven hysteria of our short-attention span that hungers for the next pending calamity to feed our social angst. We're just not happy unless life is going to hell in a hand basket.

Despite my disappointment and frustration with the impossible demands of the NOP standards, I have come to respect and comprehend the depth of the National Organic Program and why it was so badly needed in our country. I also learned some specifics along the way.

First, because producers and marketers used and abused the word, "organic," we lacked any shred of integrity, possessed no confidence, nor observed no consistency that gave either producers or consumers any common ground on what constituted organic produce. It was basically anybody's guess what the word meant, and it could mean just about anything.

Second, because the definition of organic production was left up to a personal opinion of what may or may not be allowed, the USDA stepped in to mandate what it means to be organic under the National Organic Program. Strict requirements and clear protocols sought to bring every one to the same page, in the same book.

Third, unless a producer follows the organic protocols, as lined out and strictly defined by the National Organic Program, they may not use the word, "organic," on any label or description of their produce. However, if you import a foreign product that meets the organic standards in the country of origin, you are free to label and market that product as organic in the United States, even if the country of origin's standards are less demanding than the standards in our domestic program. Do I smell a loop hole?

Fourth, except for the rare beekeepers uniquely situated in isolated, remote and unpopulated parts of the United States, free of agricultural chemicals and synthetic pesticides, the organic standards for honey production are beyond the abilities of most beekeepers. While not completely impossible, the majority of the beekeepers in the United States cannot qualify to produce organic honey. Since most of us cannot qualify, we cannot use the word, "organic." Period. No exceptions.

Fifth, for that remnant of the minority of beekeepers who can qualify and meet the organic standards, certification is required. Certification means they must keep meticulous notes and accurate records, and have those records verified by an accredited third party. An exemption of certification exists for the qualified beekeeper who markets less than $5,000 in gross sales, but does not exclude this person from keeping the rules.

Sixth, as the rules and standards for organic apiculture are still on the books as recommendations, not yet officially sanctioned, an accredited certifying agent has no firm foundation on which to qualify a beekeeping operation as organic. There are similar laws and parallel standards from other countries that may be used, presenting an inconsistency that provides a little, "wiggle room." Such inconsistencies are left up to the discretion of the certifying agent. Certification requires three years of organic production with accurate record keeping.

Seventh, to circumvent their frustration, some producers have opted to market their products as, "non-certified organic." There are no rules or regulations, in the letter of the law, that prohibit this disclaimer that seems to reside in the spirit of the law. Still, it appears misleading and deceptive as the consumer's attention will be drawn to the word, "organic," and likely will not question what it means to be certified, or not certified.

Eighth, in the end, I'm S.O.L., (Sorta Outta Luck) when it comes to being organic. In reality, I have no recourse if I desire to be legally approved as an organic beekeeper. Since my forage zones for each of my apiaries will not qualify and satisfy the rules and recommendations, I am left to manage my hives *as organically as possible*, perhaps utilizing treatment-free objectives or chemical-free management.

If I want to be organic, with or without the blessing of certification, I am still obligated to uphold and observe the recommendations of the National Organic Program. Just because I keep an organic garden on my little corner of the world, I cannot call my honey organic. I cannot control where my bees fly and what they collect. I cannot control what my neighbor sprays on his GMO rutabagas and kumquats.

Ninth, even though I take pride in managing my bees without synthetic pesticides or feeding high-fructose corn syrup, my opinion that I am an, "organic," beekeeper has no merit. Though I prescribe to Libertarian political views, though I may cringe and lament the burdensome regulatory exigencies, I am still free to keep my bees as I see fit. I just cannot use the word, "organic," because, after all, I'm not organic unless I comply with the program.

Tenth, the NOP forces me to look at the larger picture. Organic production is so much larger than what I do on my farm. The definition of what it means to be organic is not a matter of my fickle opinion or grandiose imagination. Otherwise, I'm part of that errant contingent running amok professing ignorance and merely perpetuating the problem that the NOP attempted to eliminate.

The National Organic Program is not to be perceived as some form of government oppression or censorship. It's a much needed effort to bring sanity and integrity to the market place, for both producers and consumers.

In the end, that's where it's at. I'll just have to live with it. I'm happy just to be able to keep bees.

Bottom line: I'm not an organic beekeeper, and it doesn't matter now belligerently self-righteous I become or what unconventional, apicultural path I tread, there are rules and regulations set forth to protect the consumer and bring a little integrity to those of us who would otherwise revel in our supposedly, "natural, apiary.

About the author:

Grant F.C. Gillard began keeping honeybees in 1981 following his graduation from Iowa State University from the College of Agriculture. He started out with twenty hives on the family farm in southern Minnesota and now resides in Jackson, Missouri where he tends around 200 hives...for now.

He sells honey at several local farmer's markets as well as raising his own locally adapted queen honeybees. He is a husband of twenty-eight years and father to three grown children.

He pastors the First Presbyterian Church in Jackson, Missouri, as his "day job." He frequently threatens to retire to devote his full energy to beekeeping, but secretly, he enjoys the ministry and is greatly appreciated by his congregation.

After serving for the past twenty-one years in this position, he has become more of a community chaplain and is often simply called, "The Bee Guy," or "The Honey Dude," depending upon which generation recognizes him at Wal-Mart.

He is eternally grateful to members of his congregation who have graciously allowed him to dabble in this hobby, and for his restraint of not turning every sermon into an illustration on beekeeping. He is a past-president of the Missouri State Beekeepers Association, and in 2012 received the coveted, "Beekeeper of the Year," award for his service to the MSBA.

He is a frequent conference speaker and may be contacted at: gillard5@charter.net. Contact him regarding his availability for your next event.

Other books of interest may be found at:

www.CreateSpace.com

and

http://www.Smashwords.com

Or visit Grant's personal web site where you can look at his other publications and read sample chapters:

www.grantgillard.weebly.com

(click on the "My Books" tab at the top)

You can find him on Pinterest and Facebook, or just jump on any search engine and "Google" him.

****

Special thanks go to my late father, Jack F. C. Gillard, (1928 - 2012), whose inspirations always gave us children permission to be anything we wanted to be, to do anything we wanted to do, that with the right amount of hard work, with a good education and God's help, anything was possible.

I hope to pass along that same inspiration to my children.

Other Popular Beekeeping Resources by Grant F. C. Gillard

Beekeeping with Twenty-five Hives:

From Passion to Profits

www.createspace.com/4152725

A Ton of Honey:

Managing Your Hives for

Maximum Production

www.createspace.com/4111886

Free Bees!

The Joy and the Insanity of Removing and

Retrieving Honey Bee Swarms

www.createspace.com/4107714

Keeping Honey Bees and Swarm Trapping:

A Better Way to Collect "Free" Bees

www.createspace.com/4106626

Why I Keep Honeybees

(and why you should, too!):

Keys to Your Success

www.createspace.com/4043781

Beekeeping 101:

Where Can I Keep My Bees?

www.createspace.com/4044187

Honey! It Turned to Sugar!

Dealing with Issues of Granulated Honey

www.createspace.com/4044721

Simplified Queen Rearing:

A Non-Grafting Approach Using

The "Nicot" Queen Rearing Kit

www.createspace.com/ 4542113

https://www.createspace.com/4106626

Keeping Honey Bees and Swarm Trapping

A Better Way to Collect "Free" Bees

https://www.createspace.com/4111886

A Ton of Honey

Managing Your Hives for Maximum Production

https://www.createspace.com/4107714

Free Bees!

Removing and Retrieving Honey Bee Swarms

https://www.createspace.com/4044187

Beekeeping 101: Where Can I Keep My Bees?

https://www.createspace.com/4043781

Why I Keep Honey Bees

(and why you should, too!)

https://www.createspace.com/4044721

Honey! It Turned to Sugar

Dealing with Granulated Honey

https://www.createspace.com/4111285

The Banker's Secret

Personal Finance and Debt Management

https://www.createspace.com/4147010

Better Luck **THIS** Time:

Making Good Luck Happen

Made in the USA
Lexington, KY
14 November 2015